Living on the Pearl of the Red Sea

Living on the Pearl of the Red Sea

♦

Eufrasia Gagliardo

♦

THE UNIQUE PEOPLE OF MASSAWA

©2021 Eufrasia Gagliardo

All Rights Reserved.

This book is subject to international copyright law. No part may be reproduced by any means without written permission. Inquiries should be made to the author.

Much gratitude to *Ghideon Musa Aron* for permission to use some of his amazing photos of Massawa, Eritrea.
Instagram: @ghideonmusa

Front cover photo *Sheik Seid Island* courtesy of *Ghideon Musa Aron*

Back Cover photos property of *Eufrasia Gagliardo*

Typesetting by Aishah Macgill

Cover Design by Aishah Macgill

Published by Finite Publishing
www.finitepublishing.com

ISBN 978-1-925049-36-7

To my children, Luigi, Mariangela and John-Paul who encouraged me to write this book and sustained me with their love and support through the process.

About the Author

Splitting life between the beautiful Sunshine Coast, Australia and the stunning vineyard's of Umbria, Italy, Eufrasia is now working on an anthology of poetry and other book projects.

After many joy filled years of being a mother and a grandmother, Eufrasia is now looking forward to fulfilling her life's ambition to spend some time in the *Holy Land*.

Contents

INTRODUCTION ♦
THE GIRL OF THE NEIGHBOURHOOD i
THE MYSTERIOUS HOUSE 1
THE DOCKYARD 9
THE LADY AND THE CURSE 19
THE MOTHER TERESA OF ERITREA 25
THE LADY OF MILAN 39
MODEL FOR A DAY
MODEL FOR PHOTOGRAPHER LINO PELLEGRINI 49
THE ISRAELI FISHERMEN 95
THE *JOURNALIST* 101
THE OYSTER MAN 109
THE YOUNG BRIDE AND THE BLACK PEARL 117
THE BUTTON MAN 125
THE AQUARIUM FILLER 131
THE KON TIKI 139
THE DEPUTY COMMANDER
AND THE EMPEROR 147
THE ONE 157
THE LEPROSY CRUSADERS 165
CONCLUSION ♦
THE JOURNEY CONTINUES 171
ACKNOWLEDGEMENTS 174
REFERENCES 176

Introduction

THE GIRL OF THE NEIGHBOURHOOD

I WONDER IF MY PARENTS HAD A PREMONITION THAT I would live an extraordinary life when they named me Eufrasia on October 16, 1947. If you have a curious mind like I do, you often ponder these things. I realised that without any stretch of the imagination, you could break my name down to – *Eu* is for Europe, *Fra* is for Africa and the end says *Asia*. Three different continents. My school-friends took to this with gusto, greeting me with *Ciao EuropeAfricaAsia!*

When you are given a name that is worldly and are born with an outgoing and friendly personality, you are bound to have a life that is full of adventure and intrigue. As I reflect on my life while creating this book, I marvel at how I have lived in all three of those continents and created unique and precious memories in each destination. This book is a homage to the people who have had lasting impacts on me and each chapter is a short story that pays tribute to their unique contribution to my life. I met all of these extraordinary people during my childhood and young adult life in Africa – more specifically Massawa – and I have carried their stories in my heart ever since.

I was born in Adi Ugri, a village in the south of Eritrea, located two kilometres from the city centre of Mondefera. The village of Adi Ugri, is believed to be an ancient place that was founded in the pre-Aksumite period around the fifth century B.C.E.. My family moved to Massawa in 1949, when I was two years old. Massawa is an important Eritrean port city and lies at the north of the Red Sea inland of the famous Dahlak Archipelago. Eritrea lies between Sudan and Ethiopia and opposite Saudi Arabia and Yemen. Massawa is often referred to as the Pearl of the Red Sea because it is the largest natural deep-water port on the Red Seas as well as holding an abundance of pearls, which are extracted from its surrounding reefs.

Massawa has two historical districts – each on its own island constructed on top of coral. The oldest is the Old City on Batse (Massawa) Island. A 440 metre causeway that looks like a highway floating in the water leads from Massawa to Taulud Island. Taulud was uninhabited until the late 19th century when Italians started construction there. It became the bustling business district of the region and also the home of Emperor Haile Selassie's palace. Taulud is connected to the mainland with 1030 metre long causeway.

Because of its history as a valued trade route between the Mediterranean and Indian Oceans, Massawa had been under the control of many different countries in its existence and the result was a cultural melting pot. On the island, Italians, Greeks, Muslims, French, English, Sudanese, Eritreans Arabs, Dankalis, British Indians, Abyssinians and other Red Sea peoples all lived together in harmony. I thrived in a community where different cultures, religions and customs were accepted and celebrated and I find it extremely hard to see discord and conflict in today's society when I have lived in a place where this simply didn't exist.

My father Damiano was a sailor in the Italian Navy and had been posted to Eritrea before leaving military service. He had worked on rebuilding the Catholic Church in Massawa, St Mary's, before taking on a role at the *Saline di Massawa* – the salt factory.

My father had been a prisoner of war for five-and-a-half years and was a quiet man as a result. There is no doubt he emerged from captivity as a changed man. He was not a talkative person by any stretch of the imagination. But he transformed when he listened to music. I grew up with the notes of my father's classical music records reverberating off the walls of our unique home. The gramophone was always loaded with one of his prized records.

My childhood home was a fantastical place that transported my young mind on all sorts of wild and wonderful adventures. The architecture of Massawa and

Taulud speaks volumes about its less than idyllic history, with a mash of Egyptian, Ottoman, Turkish, Arabic and Italian buildings. The colour palette of the buildings was predominantly white, giving it a distinct Mediterranean feel and the colonial embellishments added to the buildings over the years gave them a unique flavour that Massawa became renowned for.

What Massawa lacked in terms of a vibrant building colour palette, she more than made up for in the unique combination of architectural styles. The Italian colonial style was dominant and elaborate columns and latticework were everywhere on Taulud. When you combined this with the character of Arabic arches and flourishes throughout Massawa, the region had a charm that was a major drawcard for wealthy holidaymakers. The homes were Italian-inspired villas and mansions, all with high ceilings and verandas to maximise the sea breeze. In an era before air conditioning, this was vital to make the city inhabitable.

The home I grew up in had been used as a hospital during World War II and as having been born after the war, I could only imagine what would have unfolded within its walls. Of course, as a child I had a rather romanticised version of this war hospital and no real concept of the horrors that would have landed those young men in the hospital and the trauma endured by the women trained to care for them as they tended to their injuries.

Like all of the external façades in Massawa, my home was white and had large verandas that wrapped around it.

There were four enormous, square apartments inside that surrounded a central circular common area. The living area felt massive to my small frame and my parents had furnished the entire home with colonial-style pieces. The piece de resistance to me was having access to the roof. There was a big cross up there, which would have signalled to aircraft on both sides of the war of the building's status as a hospital. I would climb up and down those stairs multiple times every day and was granted a bird's eye view of the main street of Taulud.

Our house was opposite the C.I.A.A.O. (Concessione Italiana Alberghi Africa Orientale, which translates to something like Italian Hotel Concession of East Africa), and I could spend many wistful hours watching the wealthy people who would arrive there for holidays. The uniformed valet would greet them at the car and open the doors to allow the immaculately dressed women out before their husbands or boyfriends. I would make up stories about who they were and what their life of privilege was like as I watched them ascend one side of the split staircase and walk into the main reception in the middle of the building. I would marvel at their clothes and hairstyles when they would leave the hotel to go out for a walk or to dinner nearby. I also spent time counting the number of open windows of the three-storey hotel to see if I could figure out how many people were inside. Because the windows were louvred and guests pushed them right out from the building to let the breeze in, this was an easy game to play.

Unlike some of the beautiful gardens that surrounded the larger, more affluent homes in Massawa, my house didn't have much of a garden at all. It was a big job to maintain anything that wasn't a native species as the climate was so harsh and the high temperatures were a challenge for even the most talented gardener. It did, however, have an underground bunker which would have been a safe haven during those bombing raids. Having a bunker made my home even more special to me, it was a prime location for adventures, but I was much too scared to venture down there alone.

Being a site foreman at the Saline di Massawa, my father worked long hours. The first time I was able to see his workplace was on a school excursion. This trip was something every local student had the opportunity to do at some point. I remember seeing the massive salt mound rising from the ground and imagining it was actually a snow-capped mountain. This is rather comical when you consider the average temperature in Massawa is thirty degrees celsius and there were summer days when it would get to forty-five degrees in the shade.

As an outgoing kid, there were many times when I would unintentionally irritate my father. But our bond was so strong that he only had to look at me a certain way and I knew I had to quieten down. He spent the vast majority of my childhood in his Saline uniform – a khaki shirt and shorts with a colonial pit helmet. He would wake every morning at 4am and turn the radio on to catch up on all of the news from Italy, which is where he was born and raised.

Introduction ♦ The Girl of the Neighbourhood

My father was my best teacher. He helped me to understand the world around me by answering my rapid-fire questions whenever he came home. I would wonder how things worked and why things were the way they were. When I couldn't find the answers for myself, my father would be the next best source. Learning to navigate by the stars while in the navy, my Dad loved to show me the constellations and explain what part the earth played in the context of the wider universe. He was so fond of stargazing, that on the evenings when we were blessed with a cloudless sky, he would wake me up to join him on the terrace, which he had transformed into our own little observatory. He had a wealth of knowledge, and was very patient with me. The time we spend together was very special.

My mother, Mary, was Greek Maltese. She was a petite lady and I get my stature from her. With her olive complexion and stunning blue eyes, she was an exotic beauty, and it was common for people to stop her in the street to complement her on her appearance. Far from being just a beautiful woman, my mother had a very kind heart and was always looking for ways to help people. If someone she knew was sick, she would visit and cook for them, she would also volunteer to spend time at the hospital with people she didn't even know to brighten up their days. My mother could speak Italian, Greek and French and she had the most interesting hobby in the world.... She was an *Oneirocritic* – a person who interprets dreams.

My mother never used her talents professionally, but she

would offer help to friends who would come to her at all hours for advice about their dreams and for guidance on what meaning it had for their lives. I remember well the sweltering summer evenings when my mother would gather some friends and they would sit under the stars in the backyard with the sea breeze and talk about their dreams. She was uncannily accurate with what she could interpret – and by the age of ten, I knew just about everything about everyone in town from listening to their questions and the gossip that followed the deep and meaningful discussions around dreams.

My father's grounded nature was contrasted by my mother's heightened senses and her gift, so it was no wonder that I was a bit of a free spirit and a child that was not scared to be part of my neighbourhood. I was not afraid to go out and mingle or explore. I really was a girl of the neighbourhood, in fact, I was the only child my age, the other kids were either too young or too old to be playing with me. So every day, I would be my own best company, wandering around Taulud, exploring all it had to offer. I grew up speaking Italian, Greek, Arabic and Tigrigna, so I could communicate with just about everyone on the island. This was a handy skill for a free spirit like me, who was allowed to roam and explore to my heart's content with some simple boundaries in place. It was also a requirement that I was home at 1pm for lunch daily with my parents.

The community was close-knit and everybody knew me so I was always safe. I never knew what awaited me every morning as I left my home. My mother used to say, "You will never die of starvation Eufrasia, because even if you get lost, you eat all of the traditional foods from the cultures on the island and you speak the languages."

I would let my parents know which direction I would be heading off in that day and would skip down the road. With such a small and connected population, they knew I would be watched over by those around me. Because I mainly interacted with adults, I grew up very quickly.

In the summertime, my mother, myself and my little brother went inland to the mountains in Asmara, the capital of Eritrea, for some respite from the heat. My father would stay in Massawa to be closer to his work and would visit with us on weekends. The road from Massawa to Asmara winds all the way around Emba Soira, the highest mountain in Eritrea. The road climbs from sea level all the way up to 2,325 metres in just over 100 kilometres. Being partial to carsickness, I never enjoyed having to travel between the two cities. The hairpin turns along the stretch of road always made me queasy. However, whenever we took the journey at night, you could see the lights of Massawa from the top of the mountain.

I went to middle-school at Collegio Sant'Anna, a boarding school in Asmara. Because I spent the school terms in Asmara, I would choose to go back to Massawa to spend my holidays with my father. When I was under his care alone, he would insist I be accompanied by the maid on my daily adventures when he was at work.

I delighted in people watching, but more often than not, I would find myself at the beach. There was something about the soothing feel of the white sand between my toes and staring at the glistening expanse of azure waters that calmed me at the same time as igniting my imagination. As one of the most important ports on the Red Sea, ships from all around the world would come through the Suez channel to the Massawa port. Cargo ships and cruise ships from England, Norway, India and even Australia would stop by and they would cross paths with towering navy warships and traditional wooden sambuk boats owned and operated by the local Arabians and the smaller houris, which could propel a maximum of five fishermen with their small outboard motors. Unfortunately, all I could see from my location on the island were the petrol tankers, which would make their way past Taulud on their way to the AGIP depot in Massawa.

But watching the sea took on a whole new dimension at night, when the lampara – fishing boats equipped with oil lanterns – would come out. As the sky darkened, they appeared to glide gracefully across the water, luring fish to the surface with the light. Fishermen on board would then harpoon the fish, sharks, squid and anything else that dared to investigate the source of the light and either take them home to feed their families or present them for sale at the fish market the following day.

Tourists were a constant in Massawa, with many venturing out for fishing charters and sightseers flocking to Green

Island. Boats would take divers around the Dahlak Islands to explore the grand coral reefs that wrapped around the archipelago. Long before the advent of social media, there seemed to be a universal route people would walk in order to *be seen*. There was an impressive archway in front of the port people would stop and take photographs with, then they ventured to a bar at the Hotel Savoia. Walking between the port and the Hotel Savoia meant you had officially arrived and those who wanted to be noticed would have the best opportunity to make a grand entrance. The main streets had amazing shops, mostly run by Italian families, and on the other side of town, there were a string of Arabic-style cafés where you could sit on tables and chairs in the street and sip tea or coffee.

While there was an eclectic array of cultures in Massawa, the lifestyle was very European. People would work until midday and close up their businesses to return home to the family for a meal. Some chose this time to go for a swim, head out on their boats or visit Yacht Club for an aperitif. There would be ample time to rest if needed before heading back to work again at 3pm and work through until 8pm. People would then congregate together after hours and socialise. We used to change clothes three times a day; one outfit for the morning, one for the afternoon and another for the evening nightlife.

As a child, no matter where I roamed, I knew I had to be home by 1pm because my mother would have prepared lunch and it would be served at 1pm sharp. My father came home from the Saline every lunchtime and I was expected to be there to greet him. There was no getting out of it. I would often enjoy a nap after lunch, but if I was too restless to sleep, I could look at picture books or play with my toys in my room so long as I didn't disturb my parents or younger brother, who was four years younger than me.

As I grew up, the island itself became more intriguing to me. There was a real sense of community and people gathered together regularly for parities, charity events and just to socialise generally. I enjoyed the motor-sport racing, the yacht regattas, the annual Navy Day and costume parties at the CIAAO. But the primary place to gather was the Massawa Yacht Club, formerly called Lido di Massawa. It was right on the foreshore and had an impressive tidal swimming pool created by a large rock wall. Residents and visitors alike would enjoy swimming in there and exploring the marine life that came and went freely. The club, which was the première social gathering location during my years in Massawa, has since been destroyed by guerrilla warfare in the 1980s and 90s.

The open-air cinema was a favourite and there were churches and mosques for many denominations to have a place of worship. The school was run by nuns and priests. There were bars and restaurants that would overflow with tourists and residents alike. The boutique Bazaar in the middle of town had everything you needed and the outdoor Arabic souk a little further out of the main street was a bustling traditional marketplace where you could indulge all of the senses. The smells of the incense, teas and spices, the look and feel of the fabrics and clothing and the taste of the delicious food served up by the vendors. It was like someone had reached into the pages of the historic One Thousand and One Nights literary collection and brought it to life.

As the manager of the boutique bazaar in town for eight years, I came to know and love so many incredible people in Massawa and this book is a homage to them and their stories. What I found incredibly humbling is that I have been able to have relationships with so many wonderful people who were changing the world in their own unique way. When I sat down to write this book, I was surprised by how many people I could have written about, memories came flooding back and the spirits of those who had passed seemed to be tapping me on the shoulder to remind me of our time together.

Remembering them has brought me many laughs as well as many tears of both joy and sadness. I hope these stories honour those people and their legacy.

The Mysterious House

As Intriguing as I Thought my own Home was, it didn't compare to the one I would come to discover through an unlikely friend. As a curious girl with unlimited imagination, I loved looking at everything, to touch, feel and smell whatever was in front of me — and ask for explanations for anything I didn't yet understand.

There was a particular beach, which had no name, that was like a second home to me. It was a place where I would often have picnics with my parents and little brother Paolo. We would often meet family friends there and I have fond memories of my father giving me shoulder rides through the water as he was such a good swimmer. The view from the beach was astonishing because there was a breathtaking view of Mount Ghedem. It seemed so far away that it was unreachable, but looking at the lush greenery, I imagined the gazelles would roam freely on the mountain and maybe the pirates had found caves on its landscape and put their treasure inside for safekeeping.

One thing that wasn't out of range was a mansion that sat on the edge of the road and was the closest to the beach. At that time, there were very few homes by the seaside. You could call them mansions even by today's standards. All of them were owned by incredibly wealthy, high profile people. This mysterious house had a colonial style villa with verandas that overlooked the sea, but it also had a curious structure on top of the roof.

Maybe it's an outlook to watch out for pirates? Maybe you can sit there and watch the dolphins every morning and try to spot whales? Maybe you can just climb up there for peace and quiet? I would come up with something new just about every time I saw it there. Surrounded by high, white walls, I couldn't see anything below the roof-line of the house and it gave the dwelling an extra sense of mystery and excitement.

This house had me intrigued, it was a mystery that I had to explore. My imagination was fixated with the lookout on its roof and I spent my days looking for someone to show up — but they didn't. Why didn't they use this area of the house during the day? My imagination went into overdrive. If they didn't show up during the day, they must have been nocturnal — but definitely not a vampire — that was a bit too far-fetched, even for me. My best guess was the person who lived in this mystery house must have been an astronomer! That made sense to me. He would only come out at night and stargaze, like my father and I did. He would have had all sorts of telescopes, star charts and most of all I hoped he had an *Astrarium*. Now that would have been a dream come true – my dad spoke to me about the role nature had in connection with the plants and stars, but to see a real planetarium that showed the cycle of nature in a mechanical form would have been incredible. I pictured this astronomer to be a *wizard* like Mago Zurlino. He would have long hair and a thick beard with glasses, a pointy hat, and he would have liked to work in silence, as though he was suspended between the heavens and earth. I had to find out more about this house. So I kept going near – and stayed on the beach looking back – observing it for what seemed like hours. One day I was sure I would meet this mystical *wizard* and be invited to go inside this house.

There were rarely any swimmers around during the morning hours and I would mostly have the beach to myself. Without any waves or strong currents, I would frolic in the water, and being a strong swimmer, I would venture a short way into the sea to see what sort of marine life I could discover, diving down to collect seashells to add to my vast collection at home. I would also spend time following falcons when one would fly overhead, determined to follow it as far as I could to see if it would lead me to their nests.

One morning when I was five or six years old, a tall Muslim man came out from behind the wall of the mysterious house. He had a short beard and wore a pristine white kaftan that was immaculately pressed. I was beyond excited to finally get a small glimpse of what lay behind those giant walls.

"What are you doing out here? It isn't safe for a little girl to be wandering around down here," he called out as he walked towards me.

"Why? I do it every other day, so what's wrong today?"

He shook his head, "Oh no, no, no... you see, there's a big fish...."

"What big fish? I've never seen a big fish!"

"Oh, it is enormous!" He spread his arms out wide to exaggerate the size.

"He will find you in the sea and you will be the perfect size to fit right inside his mouth. He will swallow you up and take you away. Your parents will never see you again."

"Ummm, okay," I didn't really believe him and I just wanted to get back into the water.

"Please don't go swimming. Because I won't be here every time in case you get yourself into trouble," he pleaded and I could see he was genuinely worried about me.

Seeing that I was going to be stubborn about it and not heed his warning, the man invited me inside for a snack with a warm smile and said he had children at home that

I could play with. The opportunity to finally meet the people that lived in this mysterious house was too great to resist. I agreed straight away and followed him up off the beach. The mystery was finally going to be solved!

As soon as we were through the gate, I was mesmerised by everything around me. The home was absolutely beautiful, everything immaculate and in its place. The walls were trimmed with colonial wood features and all of the furniture looked delicate and expensive, but what caught my attention the most was the books. There were so many books! Lined up in bookshelves in their very own personal library complete with a solid wood desk that also had books scattered across the top.

After I'd completed a tour of the house, I realised there were no paintings or family pictures anywhere, but there were many interesting tapestries. One that captured my attention featured a winged horse with a human face. I had never seen anything like it before, so I asked the man about it.

"That is a Buraq, it brings the soul to heaven. So you see, if the big fish gets you in the sea, he will be the one who takes you to heaven," he replied with a wink.

I also noticed the very few mirrors in the home were covered in thick black drapes. I found this odd as there was no way you would be able to see anything, which is what mirrors are for! So I asked the man about that too.

"It is because Satan uses a mirror to distract you from

praying. It leads you away from your faith," he said. "When he sees that you are too busy looking at the mirror, he laughs at you."

We finished in the living area and he introduced me to his wives. I forget how many there were, but they all appeared much younger than the man and they were sitting in the spacious living area on a huge day bed with carved solid wood legs and white cushions on top. They were talking quietly over a cup of coffee and embroidering. I was disappointed to find out his children were actually babies and no good to play with at all, so I had to be content with talking to the wives.

We all became good friends and I would visit the mysterious house many times. I came to learn the man had a position high up in City Hall and the white kaftan I had seen him wearing the first time we met was somewhat of a signature outfit for him. Inside the home, I was able to see the wives without the coverings that their religion required them to wear whenever they went outside. They were so beautiful and made the most delicious food, which I was delighted to indulge in whenever I visited. The evening meals during Ramadan, which is a month of prayer and reflection observed by the Muslim community, were the most decadent. For the entire month, they would only eat a small meal before dawn, fast all day and then have a nightly feast to break the fast. I especially loved to visit for these incredible feasts.

The wives were amused by me and enjoyed my visits. They

had a special way of applying makeup and I loved having little makeovers whenever I visited. They used a powder for every element of the makeup and would create fantastic hairstyles for me as well. My mother would scream when I got home because she would then have the job of washing it all off, so it wasn't on my face for school the next day.

With all of the questions they asked me every time I came to visit, I felt like I was a bit of a mystery to them, when all along, the house and the people who lived there had been a mystery to me.

The Dockyard

The Sea was one of the most magical places for me as a child and the gateway to this kingdom in my imagination was the dockyard. The dockyard was connected to the open sea by a canal. Whenever I had free time, I would get my swimmers on and head down to the jetty to get into the water.

As soon as my toes touched the water, or I dove off the end of the jetty, I would transform into a mermaid. My human legs would morph into a fish tail with glittering scales that would reflect the sunlight in the water and I would gain the ability to hold my breath for longer than I could have as a normal girl. In my imagined mermaid form, I would spend countless hours swimming below the piers of the jetty, joining schools of sardines, watching crabs scurrying along the sea floor and trying to uncover the octopus I knew was hiding down there somewhere.

One of my favourite mermaid activities was playing hide and seek with the resident stingrays. Whenever I came splashing into the water, they would rush to settle on the bottom of the sea and cover themselves in sand, rivalling the octopus for their ability to camouflage. Whenever I brought my flippers, to become even more mermaid-like, I would be better equipped to dive down and look for the stingrays so I could annoy them. I would give them a friendly wave and try to touch their slippery skin before they were off again with a swift flap of their wing-like fins.

My underwater palace was adorned with seaweed, with varieties that grew up from the sea floor and others that would float in and out at the mercy of the tides. Seaweed made a great obstacle course for me and my fellow stingrays to navigate and created imaginary obstacles and challenges for me to solve in the day's adventures.

Sometimes, I would get lucky and a much larger manta ray would be visiting my magical realm. Watching them glide through the water with utter grace and effortlessness was a marvel for my young mind. I likened it to watching a bird soar through the skies on a gentle breeze. I was always captivated by them and would easily lose track of time in my underwater dominion.

There was one manta ray who became accustomed to having me around and no longer tried to flee from my advances. We would spend many magical moments swimming together and chasing each other. One day, she was swimming behind me and sped up, gliding into position directly on top of me! I didn't quite know how I would manage to swim out from under her to reach the surface for my next breath, but even at seven years old, my mind knew not to panic. I was a mermaid, after all, so I kept swimming until I was able to find a way out from under her. I was very short of breath by the time I reached the surface, but I was proud that I managed to find a solution on my own to get out of trouble. This remains one of my fondest memories of bonding with the wildlife in Massawa.

The only thing I was scared of was moray eels. They were like snakes of the sea and their beady eyes terrified me. I remember one day jumping from the pontoon and exploring around a piece of boat shrapnel left over from the war. There are many reefs that have been able to grow and thrive on the shipwrecks of German and Italian ships that had been bombed and scuttled. Researchers believe there are more than thirty-six vessels in the sea around Massawa, the Dahlak Islands, and Assab.

What I had discovered was only a small portion of a bow and some coral had already started to grow around it. I reached out to touch the tendrils of an anemone that was swaying gently in the water and saw a nearby pylon that was poking just above the water, so I swam over and climbed onto it. While standing on the pylon and looking around, I realised it was just about time to go back home.

But when I looked down into the water before I jumped in, I saw a moray eel and became paralysed with fear. Oh my God! How am I going to get out of this one? I looked all around me, but there was no way that I was going to get in that water knowing the eel was lurking below.

Lucky for me, there was a fisherman nearby and I called out to get his attention.

"FISHERMAN! FISHERMAN!" I yelled until he looked up, realising I was addressing him.

"What's wrong with you?" he asked.

"There is an eel down there...."

"So what?" he replied, shrugging his shoulders at me.

"I cannot swim back and I have to get back to shore because I will be in trouble with my parents. Can you help me?"

Even though he had never met me before, he didn't want to see me stranded. He gave a sigh, put down his fishing pole and dived in to get me. I was able to climb onto his back and he swam me back to the pontoon.

Whenever I had my fill of mermaid time, I would venture to the collapsed wharf and explore in the shallows around the deteriorating wood. It was a place filled with anemones and an entire ecosystem of small, colourful fish darting in and out of the crevices. This was also where the talparia ciprea exusta, a type of sea shell, could be found. It was unique to the Red Sea, making it even more magical in my eyes. Even now, seeing empty black exusta shells evokes the emotions of carefree exploration and intrigue that were firm fixtures whenever I discovered a new shell to take home. Watching the living exusta was a sight to behold. They were as black as the darkest night and when they were settled, the mantle would come out each side of the bottom of the shell and wrap so delicately around its exterior. I used to think it looked like an apple under the sea. If you looked closely, you would see the little antenna poking out the front of the shell opening. I would watch them in awe and sometimes, when I was feeling a little adventurous, I would touch the velvety mantle and giggle as it shot straight back into the protection of their shells.

When my fingers and toes became so wrinkled that I couldn't stand to be in the water anymore, I would emerge from the wharf and grow back my little girl legs and head over to the dockyard, where they built boats.

The owner of the dockyard, Camillo Simone, knew my father very well. They were born in the same town in Italy and had grown up together, reconnecting in Massawa many years later. Camillo understood my penchant for mermaid adventures in the waters nearby and he'd given me permission to stick my nose into the dockyard to have a wander around and see which projects they were working on whenever I wanted to. I also had access to his culture of pipis, which he was raising inside a long wooden crate filled with the most beautiful, pure white sand. It was the perfect height for me to be able to reach over the side and tickle the pipis, giggling as they clamped shut, often squirting a little seawater at me as they did. The only rule I had in the dockyard was that I had to stay clear of danger. I laugh now at how generic this rule was, but I never touched anything that looked dangerous, so it worked for us!

The dock was scattered with hundreds of planks of wood of all shapes and sizes. The smell of timber would combine with the potency of the chemicals used to bind the wood together and make it watertight, resulting in a pungent aroma that was unique to this part of Massawa.

Camillo's dockyard was renowned for making farriers, a type of sailboat, one and two-masted yachts and outboard motorboats. Although his work was very physical, Camillo had a belly that refused to budge, but added to his charm. He was always wearing some kind of hat to cover up his baldness and his friendly face was always a welcome sight when I was exploring his *castle*.

I marvelled at how skilful Camillo was and watched in awe as the boats evolved from simple materials scattered across the workshop floor to watertight vessels that towered above me. I would guess which colours they would be painted and was filled with joy when they were prepared to be launched and set off on their maiden voyage. It was like watching children grow up and be set free to explore the world on their own.

The fact that the vessels were eased ever so gently by winch into the water on top of my mermaid kingdom made it all the more special to me. I would often follow them, either on the jetty or swimming alongside in the water, as the boats experienced their first few moments of life on the sea with their new captain at the helm.

I'd imagine the vessel sailing to distant islands lined with tropical palm trees and having its underbelly tickled by hermit crabs as it docked and allowed its passengers to have the luxury holiday of a lifetime. I'd seen many a family sail to Massawa for such a holiday, so it was only natural the same thing would happen for these new boats.

One afternoon Camillo summoned me. This had never happened before in all the years I had been exploring his grounds. What have I done wrong? I must be in big trouble! I racked my brain but couldn't come up with any reason why I might have upset him. I was terrified I might be banned from this explorer's haven, so I took my time walking up to his office.

As I shuffled inside, I could see from his body language that he was not mad or upset with me. He sat calmly on a chair with a smile spread across his weathered face and I felt like I could breathe again.

"Eufrasia! You know that latest boat you have been watching me make from the beginning? It's almost ready."

He was talking about the Carolina, which he had named after his mother. It was a decent-sized ferrier and I thought it was his most beautiful yet.

"Yes...." I answered, still not sure why he needed to tell me specifically that this project was almost finished.

"Would you like to be the Godmother of the Carolina?"

I froze, completely shocked by what I had just been offered. His smile widened even more when he saw my reaction and it gave me time to recover enough to enthusiastically nod my head and reply, "Of course I will!"

That afternoon as I made my way home, I had visions of me, who was only just pushing one metre tall, trying to christen this vessel in the traditional way and failing. I thought I would not have the strength to break the bottle of champagne against the bow of the boat on the first attempt. As a girl of the island, I knew the maritime folklore that says failure to properly christen a vessel will bestow bad luck upon the boat and its passengers. How can I be responsible for that? Why did he ask me to do this?

What had started out as an exciting opportunity had quickly morphed into a source of stress and anxiety for my young mind. I spoke to my mother about it and she invited me instead to think about the wonderful life Carolina would have on the open ocean. This was the perfect distraction and I daydreamed about her arriving at piers all over the world with a happy family on board.

When the big day came, I dressed in my Sunday finest and my parents accompanied me to the dockyard where Carolina was poised majestically beside the water, ready to make her grand entrance. I was so short, I couldn't even reach the bottom of the boat, so they created a special platform for me to stand on. Camillo had also rigged up a pulley system so I could simply swing the champagne bottle back on a string and let go. The momentum would carry it towards the boat and hopefully smash, properly blessing the Carolina.

The moment of truth had come.

I gripped the bottle tight and close my eyes so I could concentrate with all my might on breaking that bottle. My father grabbed onto my legs as he saw me do this and it was just as well, because I pulled back on that string as hard as I could and I probably would have toppled over backwards. I thrust the bottle forward with all of the strength I could muster. Bang! My eyes were still squeezed shut as I heard the glass shattering on the bow of the boat and I was instantly showered with champagne.

Beaming with pride, I opened my eyes to loud applause and as Carolina was winched into the water, I saluted her with a loud, "Bon voyage Carolina!"

It wasn't long after this that I began to attend boarding school outside in nearby Asmara and my days of wandering down to the dockyard and imagining my life as a mermaid ceased. But my connection to Camillo was firmly cemented. In fact, he went on to become one of the bestmen at my wedding!

The Lady and the Curse

I Always Believed Magic was Everywhere in Massawa. But there was an undercurrent of magic throughout the island and its culture that ran much deeper than the magic I created in my own imagination. The belief of both good and evil magic runs deep in African roots. This was epitomised by the powerful image captured by photographer Kurt Lubinski in Massawa during my time on the island. It depicts two Somali women eating outside on the street, with one of the women covering her face with a blanket in order to ward off the *evil eye*.

In my young mind, I believed in guardian angels, good fairies and bad fairies, but never gave much thought to witchcraft. I never saw any old women with black pointed hats and warts on the end of their noses who regularly stirred large black cauldrons and dropped ingredients such as bat wings and newt eyes into it. I didn't think people had the power to curse others, but that changed somewhat when I met Signora Vigo. The gossip on the town grape vine was that she was the victim of a curse, a spell that someone had cast on her most likely out of jealousy.

With mixed-race parents, Signora Vigo was a beautiful woman who had an effortless air of elegance about her. Her black, curly hair was cut into a stylish bob and her eyes were as black as her shimmering locks. She seemed to float as she moved about town and to the outside world, she appeared to have it all. Her adoring husband was the manager of the Aquaduct and held a powerful position in society as an attractive and affable man. Their love story was the stuff of fairy tales and they had raised five gorgeous children who were all grown up and making their own way in life.

The Vigos owned the first car in Massawa and mingled with the elite members of society. Signora Vigo was a renowned dressmaker and was always adorned in unique, stylish gowns and beautiful stiletto shoes. She was wearing one of her signature outfits as she strolled casually through the main street in Massawa with her husband. The tap-tap of her heels on the paved streets was halted unexpectedly and replaced with a guttural scream when a loose window shutter fell from the first storey of a building.

In the freak incident, the shutter connected with Signora Vigo's nose, severing it completely from her face. The shutter came to rest across the tops of both of her feet, disfiguring her further by detaching the top half of both of her feet. If the wooden shutter had fallen off a few seconds later, Signora Vigo would have been killed. However, many would have considered her fate worse than death. With no access to plastic surgery in those times, Signora Vigo was left with terrible scarring and two holes where her nose had once been. From the moment she was discharged from hospital, her life was never the same again. Forced to face the looks of pity and the whispers of passers-by speculating who may have been jealous enough of her to cast such a wicked spell on her, she traded her glamorous and highly social life for one of isolation.

Those who were partial to speculation and didn't know Signora Vigo or the detail of the incident decided that she was the victim of a curse. My family were friends with the Vigos and I knew the whole story. I didn't believe Signora Vigo would have done anything wrong enough to deserve the wrath of a bad fairy. To me, it was simply a terrible accident.

Signora Vigo could have ventured out with a veil to hide her disfiguration, but her feet were so badly damaged that she could no longer wear the stilettos that had brought her so much joy. The town shoemaker did the best that he could for her, designing special shoes that would allow her to walk. The shoemaker was a gentle soul and embellished her shoes with beautiful elements so when she looked at her feet and saw them, she may be less inclined to break down in tears as she often did when she dared to cast her eyes towards what was left of her feet.

The Vigos owned an impressive seaside villa so she could take a few steps outside and be able to swim in the sea without being noticed by anyone. Signor Vigo provided for her so she could make a new life at home and he would do anything she wished so she would be happy. Their love and devotion for one another was unshakeable despite the horrific accident.

He built her a zoo so she could have dik-diks, a subspecies of gazelle found in Eritrea, in her garden. She also had a cheetah, ducks, birds and many species of parrots to care for. A fountain in the middle of the small zoo was a beacon for the native birds, who would flock there to bathe and rest in the sweltering hot summer days. It was her little paradise.

I daydreamed about how magical it would be to spend days among the animals like Signora Vigo did and as a talented seamstress, she spent many hours creating things to beautify her home. But even then, I realised it was her prison as much as it was her haven.

I was never scared of Signora Vigo and would regularly visit her with my mother in the evenings just to talk. The three of us would sit together on the veranda and soak up the cool, salty sea breeze and listen to the rustling of the palm leaves. We could see the big tankers were docking at the AGIP deposit at Archico bay and while looking across the channel, the lights of the employee's houses would flicker on as they arrived home for the evening. When the nights were clear, you could see the car headlights winding their way around Archico. I remember the serenity of those moments often being punctuated by the abrupt squawks of her parrots, often startling me so much I would jump out of my seat.

Signora Vigo taught me how to sew and offering for me to come over any time for a meal when I complained about what my mum was cooking for dinner that night. She would create the most delicious meals and had a flair for creativity in the kitchen that matched her finesse as a seamstress. With her five children already grown up and three already moved back to Italy, I became her new baby to care for.

When I turned seven, the time had come for me to prepare for my first Holy Communion. During one of my regular visits, Signora Vigo turned to me and said in her quiet voice, "I would like to sew your Holy Communion dress, little one." To say I was excited about this is an understatement. I had always marvelled at her elegance and grace, even after the accident, and whenever I looked at her, still dressing in her incredible gowns at home, I pictured her swanning into a ballroom with all eyes on her. I never noticed her missing nose or the stumps where her feet had once been. All I saw was an undeniably beautiful woman.

Visions of being a mini-Vigo at my Holy Communion swirled through my head as she kept me updated on how she was progressing with my dress. I was less than one-metre tall, but when she presented me with the stunning gown adorned with lace trimming and details, I felt like a princess.

Feeling like a million dollars on the day of my Holy Communion, wearing Signora Vigo's dress and a headpiece custom made by another artist in Asmara, I proudly took my first communion among my peers. My parents hosted a small party at our home to celebrate and when we heard an unexpected knock at the door, I threw open the doors to find Signora Vigo. She had walked with great pain from her home to ours and braved the stares and judgement of others to be there for me that day.

It was the most beautiful gift and one that feels as powerful today as it did for me all those years ago. It brings tears to my eyes even to this day. For that afternoon, she was out of her self-imposed prison and she had done that out of pure love for me.

The Mother Teresa of Eritrea

There was a strong religious presence in Massawa during my youth. The Catholic and Coptic Orthodox churches were within a few blocks of each other in Taulud, the mosque was near the market in Massawa, and all would be filled with devoted worshippers on their respective holy days every week. As was the case with many boarding schools of the time, I was educated by nuns and there were nuns assisting doctors and surgeons in the hospital, which I visited regularly with my mother.

My mother was such a caring woman and she would volunteer her time visiting patients who didn't have friends or relatives nearby to keep them company. Before I was old enough to go to school, she would often bring me along and I would spend many hours entertaining patients with my boundless energy and knack for being able to tell an incredibly imaginative story.

When I wasn't helping Mum to fetch things for the patients to make them more comfortable or distracting them with a recollection of my adventures around Massawa, I would see the nuns in action, rushing around to help everyone and still finding the time to show compassion and empathy for each patient they tended to. I thought one day, I will become a nun and work in a hospital to save lives too.

My imagination was limitless and, in my daydreams, I used to impersonate the nuns. To make it all believable for myself I would act it out at home too. I would make a big veil out of whatever clothing or fabric was nearby and imagine I was a nurse treating people and caring for them. I would make their rooms beautiful with flowers and ask them if they wanted something particular to eat that day, maybe something that wasn't on the standard menu just so they would feel extra special. I would set up my own clinic and treat my teddies and dolls. I imagined myself as an elderly woman with a kind face and a youthful energy that belied my physical age and I would tend to my stuffed patients with endless compassion. I would go out of my way to please my *patients* and they would always recover and leave with a happy ending thanks to the medications and prayers I gave them.

It's funny how I never dreamed of being a school nun – perhaps I didn't like the sound of them too much! Memories of these games and the nun I dreamed of growing to be remained with me for years after I started school.

During my holidays in Asmara with my mother, I received a phone call from my father telling me the elderly father of his work colleague was in hospital near where I was staying. His name was Signor Bonifacio and his relatives were too far away to visit regularly and he was getting lonely in the hospital without company outside of those charged with his care. I had met Signor Bonifacio, his wife and son many times before in Massawa and my heart went out to him that he was unwell and away from his family.

"Please can you go and see him Eufrasia?" my father asked. It was an easy decision to say, "Yes."

Familiar with the hospital environment and never shy to strike up a conversation with strangers, I knocked confidently on the door and waltzed into Signor Bonifacio's room like I was a member of staff and introduced myself. Signor Bonifacio looked frail, but smiled when I started speaking, clearly over the moon he had a visitor even though he didn't know me at first.

"So, what would you like me to do for you?" I asked with an open heart, waiting to hear how I could be of service.

"I would fancy some lollies if you could bring me some?"

It was not a request I had been expecting, but I nodded my head with conviction, knowing my mother would be happy to pay for them as I had no money myself.

"And a newspaper? I would love it if you could then sit here and read the newspaper to me."

"With pleasure!"

Signor Bonifacio was visually impaired and I liked to read and I liked lollies, so it was the perfect job for me. As I expected, my mother gave me some money to buy the supplies I needed and I rushed back to the hospital to hand over the lollies and pulled a chair closer to the bed so I could begin to read the newspaper aloud.

This was a routine I carried out every afternoon I was on holidays, going to the shops for lollies and a newspaper and going to sit with Signor Bonifacio. He was my first real life patient. I would adjust his pillow so he was comfortable and let him pick his favourite lollies before I grabbed a few and settled down on the chair to read to him.

It was during one of those fateful visits that I met her. She appeared in the doorway to Signor Bonifacio's room and I was both startled and elated to see she was the epitome of everything I daydreamed I would become when I was an older nun. It was as if I was staring into the materialisation of my dream. From the moment she appeared, an instant calm fell over the room and there was an aura of safety that emanated from her. She had beautiful deep blue eyes that were as bright as the sky on a sunny day and a smile that was wide and welcoming.

Her name was Suor Pia (Mother Pia).

I knew from that very moment she would play an important role in my life. Suor Pia was the surgeon's assistant as well as a qualified midwife and I came to learn that she had worked at the Massawa Hospital before relocating to this private clinic in Asmara. Suor Pia ran operations at the clinic and was an extremely busy woman.

I was already enjoying my time with Signor Bonifacio, but the presence of Suor Pia in the halls made my time as a holiday hospital volunteer positively life changing. I would bask in the positive energy that radiated from Suor Pia and delighted in spending time with her. She treated every person, no matter their age, as her child. She was a mother to all of us and had infinite compassion. She truly possessed a holy spirit and even when I occasionally saw her rushing down the hall post-surgery or delivery with her green scrubs smatted with droplets of blood, there was nothing shocking about the vision. In fact, in my eyes, the blood almost transformed into miniature floral blooms because their presence was proof that she had just worked hard to either save someone's life or to bring a new life into the world.

Such was the depth in which she touched my soul, I kept in touch with Suor Pia and ours was a friendship that spanned more than four decades. I had the honour of having Suor Pia deliver my eldest child, Luigi, and when I was no longer living in Massawa, we communicated regularly through letters.

In a very rare occurrence, Suor Pia became Luigi's Godmother. In order for her to accept the role, she had to seek special permission from the Archbishop as nuns are not usually permitted to become Godmothers. I knew the Archbishop myself, but Suor Pia had to seek the approval and was able to secure it. To this day, I have no idea what she presented to him to get his holiness to agree, but I am forever grateful that she had this special connection to our family.

In 1975, tensions were rising in Asmara with guerrilla warfare spearheaded by the Eritrean Liberation Front, which forced the closure of the clinic Suor Pia was working in. Undeterred, Suor Pia was driven to continue her tireless work and found another location in a less prosperous area, where the population was growing due to the displacement of the people.

The economic and political climate meant access to medication and supplies was scares and without the backing of a private practice, Suor Pia's volunteer-run clinic had to innovate to find ways to be able to treat and care for the people most in need. Spurred to action, Suor Pia reached out to connections in her hometown in Italy to create a steady supply of donations including everything from medicines and bandages to clothes and food.

Suor Pia was a conduit for this line of solidarity and everything that was donated to the clinic, she gave freely to her patients, never charging them for care and support. I remember during one of my visits to Asmara, I visited Suor Pia's clinic. A straw basket containing a couple of zucchinis, an egg, some fruit and a small amount of money sat on the reception desk. There was a note attached to the side of the basket that read – *There is no bill here, but if you feel more comfortable, any offer is welcome.*

Despite the often desperate circumstances some of the patients found themselves in, scraping together every day just to be able to feed themselves and their families, Suor Pia understood that pride was still important to understand and respect. By allowing patients to give what they could if they felt like they wanted to offer something in exchange for the service she was providing, she allowed them to keep their dignity firmly intact.

When the guerrillas arrived in Asmara, the sisters moved to Nefesit, a small town thirty kilometres east of Asmara. The road between the Asmara and Massawa is a masterpiece of Italian engineering, rising from sea level up to 2325 metres above the sea level along a series of winding bends. I had the experience of venturing along that road and have vivid memories of the awe-inspiring landscape below, the lush trees and the view stretching all the way out to Massawa, which was nestled on the seashore on the horizon. The nuns set off on a journey from Nefesit to Ghinda, which is reached by travelling on the road to Massawa.

They set off on dusk dressed in their finest white robes. A couple of members in the group were carrying the Monstrance, a sceptre that contains the holy communion host, and the group were joyfully chanting, singing and praying as they proceeded along the road.

The nuns were startled when a group of armed men jumped out from behind some nearby bushes and ordered them loudly to halt. Suor Pia recalled all of this in a letter to me and the way that she described the event gave me chills. The nuns gathered together, protecting the Monstrance, but they were shaking with fear, unsure of the intentions of these men who appeared to be part of the guerrilla movement.

Suor Pia said she prayed to God and surrendered to the situation. She knew her fate lay in God's hands and was willing to do whatever was required of her. "If God wills it, this could be our day."

The man at the front of the group barked a series of questions in Italian while holding his gun in a menacing fashion directly at the nuns.

"Where are you going?"

Suor Pia boldly stepped forward from the group, her resolve steely and her confidence high, trusting she had the protection of her Lord.

"We are walking to the monastery."

"What are you carrying? Are you concealing anything?"

"Oh, that is our God, the host. Please signor, we are just singing and celebrating our God, we are not doing anything against the law."

At this, the man softened, his shoulders slumped and be dropped his gun, ordering the rest of the men to do the same. There was a profound silence as the two groups, a peaceful group of women and a squadron of men preparing for war, looked at each other.

Within seconds, the leader of the men dropped to his knees in front of Suor Pia and bowed his head. "My God, you brought me into this life, please bless me because I am going to die."

Suor Pia rested a hand on his head and the nuns said a prayer for him and his comrades. When he stood again, there were tears in the corners of his eyes and the mood had completely shifted between the two groups. They were all simply human beings.

"We will escort you to Ghinda so you reach your destination safely," he declared with a renewed sense of purpose and the men fell into formation to flank the nuns as they continued with their procession.

Suor Pia began to dedicate her time to caring for and nurturing the orphans of Asmara and it was in this vein that she was called by God to relocate to Ethiopia. I kept a lot of her letters, they remain in my home in Italy, and this was from a letter she sent to me dated March 7, 1983.

My dearest Eufrasia,

I will shortly depart Asmara and my destination will be the south of Ethiopia. I will be leaving at the end of this month. I will be staying in Addis Ababa (the capital of Ethiopia) for a short period until I can master the language. From there, I will be going on the region of Sidama near Awassa. It is thirty-five kilometres from the border with Somalia.

I am leaving behind me a crying generation and I am going into the unknown. Yet my heart is open to every situation, and I will say to God and my Father that I am ready. I am ready for whatever

I need to be facing and I am considering all that happens to be a gift from Him.

I have faith that the Lord will be waiting for me on the way home. I am relying on the prayers of all the good people from home who love me. Please give my regards to Don Antonio (the Parish priest) let him know of God's plan for me, of which I hope to be worthy.

I hug you with all my heart,

Your Pia.

She also sent little letters to Luigi and Mariangela.

My dear Luigi,

All of the boys I meet on my way will remind me of you. I see you in all of their faces and it is like you are with me.

Please remember me in your prayers and pray also for the children.

Suor Pia.

To Mariangela,

One of the most rewarding things for a missionary nun is being mother to those who haven't got a mother. I beg you to say a prayer for all my little children.

A big hug,
Suor Pia.

In the Sidama region, Suor Pia began to truly flourish. Like a flower finally able to blossom to its full beauty, she was able to expand her mission to help orphaned children while still using her medical skills to heal the sick. She was just like Mother Teresa. She became a mother to everybody, and her warm and welcoming smile lit up the souls of so many people both young and old. While she nourished and strengthened people's spirits with her unwavering devotion to their recovery, she also had the benefit of medicines to cure their physical ailments.

In her correspondence, she shared how she cared for a 94-year-old man who was in his final days of life. She described him as being ethereal, serene and at peace even though he lay on a simple straw mat in his modest hut with nothing but a wrap draped over his body. His only source of warmth came from a rudimentary heater made from an oil tin that had been cut in half to house a single lump of coal. The burning embers from the coal were just enough to stave off the chill in the night air. Each time she visited, Suor Pia would pray with the man, ensure he was as comfortable as possible and remove the ash from a small opening to ensure the coal's embers would not be extinguished.

In a hut nearby, a young woman was living with her seven children. Her name was Elematu. She was only twenty-seven years old, but she knew God was calling her home and she did not have long left to spend with her family. Suor Pia arrived one day to find all seven children forming a halo around their mother's head, watching over her as she struggled to take each breath. Elematu no longer had the strength to talk, but as Suor Pia held her hand, her eyes told her everything she needed to know take care of my children, I am entrusting them to you to be their mother, to love them and raise them as I can no longer.

Suor Pia was with Elematu until the end, supporting her and ensuring she felt at peace and ready to meet God in heaven. The children knew they were in safe hands with her and just like the many other children she was raising, Suor Pia became their mother and gave them everything she had.

Those modest huts in Awasa may have been made from misshapen bricks and clay, but to Suor Pia they were as majestic as the most beautiful cathedrals in the world. They were the places where miracles of life and death were seen every single day. God was with these people all the time because Suor Pia was there. She worked tirelessly to see Elematu's children, and many other orphans, grow up and become educated young people who, with the nurturing influence of Suor Pia as their guardians, became empowered and driven to help their community any way they could.

We lost her much too soon, however, as her enormous, generous heart betrayed her one day and her health began to fail. She was sent back to Italy for treatment and the moment she recovered, she begged to go back to Ethiopia to continue her work. Her heart was with the orphans and every day she was away from them was even more painful than the heart attack that had separated her from them.

The congregation argued that she was no longer capable of maintaining her level of work. With another spark of the determination that had served her well in life, Suor Pia went to the very top – Pope John Paul II. She wrote him a letter that was straight to the point.

> *His Holiness,*
>
> *Please let me go back to Ethiopia. You are the only person that can allow me to go back.*
>
> *My wish is to be there with my people and to one day be laid to rest under the sky at the foot of the big Bao Bao Tree near my orphanage amongst the people I have cared for all my life.*
>
> *By the grace of God,*
>
> *Suor Pia.*

She was granted her wish and spent the rest of her time on earth doing what gave her the most joy – serving others. The ripple effect of Suor Pia's actions will be felt for generations. I believe with all my heart that her love and influence on the lives of the people she worked with is aligned with that of Saint Mother Teresa of Calcutta, although she was never acknowledged in the same way.

The Lady of Milan

While writing this book, news reports circulated the globe of how the Italian ambassador Luca Attanasio and the carabiniere (paramilitary police officer) Vittorio Iacovacci were killed in a gunfight as they travelled in a UN convoy in the Democratic Republic of Congo. Once the shock of the situation settled down, my memory was transported back to Massawa and to one person in particular – Signora Teresa Piccioni.

She was also an Italian diplomat and although this happened some forty years ago in a different part of the world, her kidnapping is something that has remained with me as a story that I felt needs to be told.

Teresa was born in Milan to an upper-class family and she enjoyed a childhood of privilege in a beautiful home filled with stately furniture, brocade curtains and crystal chandeliers. She wanted for nothing and had a maid who would answer the door and escort guests in for social gatherings or work meetings in her father's office, which was where he spent the majority of his time. As all of the girls of her pedigree did, Teresa went to a private school and enjoyed lessons from a private music tutor to hone her piano techniques, an instrument ideal for her long and slender fingers.

To escape the oppressive heat of the Milan summers, Teresa and her family would escape to their holiday home in the Italian countryside and enjoy months under the shade of established fruit trees and wandering through the woods on foot. The sounds of nature were all around her as she cycled along the bumpy country paths and delighted in the change of pace these holidays provided.

As Teresa grew up, she blossomed into a breathtakingly beautiful woman with vibrant green eyes and an air of elegance about her every movement. She was highly intelligent with a quick wit and knew how to stand on her own two feet. She completed a degree to become a qualified accountant before catching the eye of a handsome military man.

They were married and moved to Eritrea after her husband received a posting there. Teresa was pleased to find some similarities in the lifestyle in this foreign country as well as being able to use her native tongue and be understood by everyone in her new city.

Teresa had two children, a boy and a girl, but as the children grew, her marriage began to fail and she separated from her husband. There may have been tensions between Teresa and her family when she chose to marry and move to another country for love because although her ex-husband returned to Italy, Teresa remained in Eritrea with her children as a single mother.

Not one to be discouraged by a little hard work, Teresa knew she would be able to support her young family on her own and found a job as the accountant for a company that specialised in salvaging shipwrecks. Two brothers from Genoa owned the company and were also the owners of the Ghedem Hotel, which was located in Taulud. Teresa ended up managing both the salvage business and the hotel, cementing herself as an indispensable employee for the brothers.

The Ghedem Hotel was the very picture of luxury. Holidaymakers and high-flying businesspeople would land in Massawa and make their way to the hotel to experience its elegance. Those who chose to stay within the walls of the hotel had their every need catered for, with bars and restaurants with full bar service. It was no wonder the hotel was always busy, and it was common for it to be almost bursting at the seams every Easter and Christmas time.

With permanent full-time work, Teresa never had to worry about being able to provide for her children. She revelled in her independence and never felt like she needed to find a man to make her life whole again. But, as fate would have it, she would soon meet the man with whom she would spend the rest of her life. Her new husband became a true father to her children and they raised them together.

Teresa saved up her excess funds and was able to purchase the Bazaar in the middle of Massawa. It was an investment as well as providing an option for her daughter to run the business one day should she choose to. But by the time her daughter finished school, she had her sights firmly fixed on becoming a teacher and had no interest whatsoever in being a business owner. Always the supportive mother, Signora Teresa respected her daughter's wishes and despite my young age, chose to employ me to manage the shop for her. It was in the centre of town and a place where just about everyone went to at least once during the week. It sold everything from books and newspapers from around Europe, gifts and jewellery to everyday supplies. I had an assistant, Abdalla Ezi, who would set up the displays, clean and tidy up and open and close the shop. I was responsible for everything else from stock levels to customer service and balancing the books.

My childhood daydreams of becoming a nun at a hospital had transformed into aspirations of becoming a teacher as I became closer to finishing high school. But I loved being around people. Nothing lit me up more than being able to get to know someone and receive little glimpses into their incredible lives. While I always had a fondness for children, there is something about connecting with people from all walks of life that made the Bazaar the perfect job for me.

Shortly after Signora Teresa's daughter became a qualified teacher, she fell in love and became engaged, sparking planning for one of the most impressive weddings I had ever heard of – the kind where guests are still talking with excitement about it years later. Although I was not among the guests, as I had to remain in Massawa to run the shop, I heard those lucky enough to secure an invite to the black tie event were treated to high-class food and drinks at the best hotel in Asmara. Her brother, who was studying at the Bocconi University of Milan and usually came to visit his mother and sister once a year, made an appearance. He went on to become a space engineer.

Teresa's business acumen and high profile led to her securing the role of Acting Italian Consul in Massawa. It was a position she was born to have, and she excelled in supporting Italian residents who were trying to get back to Italy and ensuring those who remained were safe and well cared for.

Her daughter's wedding was just a taste of what Teresa's official parties would look like. Every year on June 2, the Festa della Repubblica – Italy's official day of celebration – Teresa would host the most impressive events. Every Italian was invited to come along to be spoiled with great food, wine and entertainment all at the expense of the Italian Government. Teresa would also be front and centre at the annual Navy Day, where naval ships from all over the world would dock in Massawa and their crew would take part in an official military parade through the streets. Dozens of nations would send representatives for that one day of celebration and the kaleidoscope of people who lived in Massawa would line the streets to clap, cheer and dance. I remember these occasions; I would relish the chance to get a glimpse of the enigmatic Emperor as he was driven by as part of the convoy – his face always fixed into a stern expression to convey his power.

With her son studying abroad and her daughter newly married and no longer living at home, I became a surrogate daughter to Teresa. We would talk often and she would invite me to events she hosted outside of the Bazaar hours, expanding my social connections and allowing me to step into a world of powerful people, even if it was for only a few hours at a time.

As there was no official hairdresser in town, I would dye her hair, put it into rollers and style it for her important events as well as ensure her nails and makeup were always on-point. This closeness resulted in a bond that lasted for the rest of Teresa's life as she sadly passed away before I could release this book.

I admired Teresa. She had an air of power about her, yet still managed to bring a touch of elegance to each of these major events and was an effortless host of other international ambassadors, council members and military leaders in her private residence, which was part of the estate of the Italian Government. Her seaside home was a beautiful two-storey villa with a garden out the back that could rival some of the best in the world. She was always hosting someone of note or organising smaller events for the rest of the community. To me, it was as if there was nothing she couldn't do.

But sadly, the political situation was deteriorating in the 1960s as the Eritrean Liberation Front (Fronte di Liberazione Eritreo) became more organised and began their armed campaign to seek Eritrea's independence from Ethiopia. Led by Hamid Idris Awate, guerrilla warfare with the government began in 1961 and escalated to the Ethiopian Civil War, which began in September 1974 when the Marxist Derg staged a coup d'état against Emperor Haile Selassie.

I remained in touch with Teresa long after I left Massawa in 1971, so I became increasingly worried for her safety. One night, my worst fears came to fruition. A small group of guerrilla soldiers docked their small boat in Massawa under the cover of darkness. There were no guards at the port as Massawa was a safe haven, usually far away from the fighting. With no police presence at the residence, the soldiers were able to break into Teresa's home, which was right near the shore, and make their way up to her second-storey bedroom.

Teresa and her second husband woke with a start to find close to ten armed men in their room with their faces covered.

"Shhhhh," one of the men cautioned with his finger pressed firmly to his lips.

"Do not panic. We don't wish to harm you. We need to take you with us."

With startled eyes, Teresa looked at her husband and knew immediately what she needed to do. However, she was too terrified to get out of bed. As she lay in a state of total shock, her life flashed before her eyes and she wondered if she would ever have the chance to hug her children or very young grandchildren ever again.

"Either you come willingly, or we will force you and we can't promise that you won't get hurt if you choose the latter. If you come with us, now, it will be better to do that and you will come to no harm," the man continued.

His tone was even, almost soothing, and Teresa could feel that he was telling the truth. She knew this wasn't about her. It was a power play and a way for the guerrillas to get media coverage through her kidnapping.

Her husband stood first, declaring boldly, "I'll go too."

"We don't have a need for you," the man shot back.

"I am not letting you take her away from me. If she agrees to come, I will come willingly also. We won't make a big fuss, wake up the neighbours or alert the police. I am willing to follow your orders, I just won't let her go with you alone. That's the deal."

By this stage, Teresa had got out of bed and started to put on some warmer clothes to stave off the night time chill she would be faced with once they left the comfort of their home.

After considering the situation for a moment, the man nodded. "Fine, two is better than one."

They gave Teresa a kaftan to put over her dress so she would be less likely to be recognised and one of the men gave his jacket to her husband. In the still night air, they were whisked back to the dock and loaded onto the boat as captives. She told me of arriving at a strange location and being taken to a secluded base by camel.

It wasn't long before news headlines around the world reported the capture Signora Teresa, the Italian acting consul. I saw one of those headlines while I was in Nigeria and my heart felt heavy as I prayed for her safety. She was captive for several weeks before being released unharmed and in one of her letters to me, she detailed how she spent many nights sleeping in the open under guard, wondering is this the end of my life?

Her captor was true to his word and they were provided with food and blankets to keep warm as they stared up at the stars during sleepless nights. But there was no comfort in knowing they were living in captivity; their freedom had been stripped away from them and they were very much at the mercy of their abductors.

Despite being relentlessly pursued by the media upon her release, Teresa chose to never give any interviews. It is no surprise Teresa and her husband decided to leave Massawa, and she stepped down from the role that had brought her so much joy prior to the kidnapping. They built their new life in Savona, northwest Italy. Being a port city, the lifestyle was very similar to the one they had come to love in Massawa and they lived out the rest of their days in peace.

MODEL FOR A DAY
MODEL FOR PHOTOGRAPHER
LINO PELLEGRINI

SEEING THE RICH AND FAMOUS WALKING THE streets of Massawa was a sight that I became used to growing up on an island that was a playground for those with wealth and prestige. But I was too young to appreciate the enormity of having Italian actress Sophia Loren spend three months in Massawa to film one of her first cinematic roles. She starred in *Africa sotto i mari*, which was released as *Woman of the Red Sea* in English-speaking countries.

Sophia played the troublesome daughter of an American millionaire who sneaks aboard his yacht destined for a deep sea diving expedition in the Red Sea and ends up falling in love with the captain. Massawa was chosen as a live set destination for its quintessential colonial aesthetics and multi-cultural population.

The cast and crew, including Sophia, stayed at the CIAAO Hotel, which I could see from my house. There is every chance I may have seen her coming in or out of the hotel during those three months in 1952 on the way to the movie sets, but I was too young to care about such things at the time.

The majority of the filming was done aboard the yacht, with some scenes in downtown Massawa, under the watchful eyes of director Giovanni Roccardi and assistant director Nanni Loy (Giovanni Loy). It was one of the first international films Sophia Loren starred in and I am proud that Massawa had but a small role to play in her becoming a multiple Oscar winner – one of the few Italian actresses to achieve such acclaim – in her future career.

It was many years later, after I had started working in the Bazaar in town, when I had my own small brush with fame with renowned journalist and underwater photographer Lino Pellegrini. Lino was an extensive traveller and came to Massawa on more than one occasion. The first time he took a boat out to Green Island and was documenting life around the Red Sea, he returned again many years later and searched off the coast of Massawa to find the wreck of the destroyer Nullo, sunk during the war by the British. He managed to find it and bring the remains to the surface.

Green Island is traditionally known as Sheikh Saeed in honour of the mosque built by its Saudi Arabian namesake in the 1400s. All that remains are the ruins of what was once a majestic place of worship, but the crumbled columns and rich Muslim history are only a small part of what attracts people to Green Island. The crystal clear azure sea sweeps calmly around the white sand beaches, cradling countless large natural rock formations that are scattered along the coastline. The soft hills offer only a smattering of greenery, but nevertheless, is home to pelicans, seagulls, kingfishers and an abundance of sea life, including playful turtles. Its wild beauty transports you to another time and place. Muslim pilgrims still venture to the mosque to pray and Italian and Eritrean families flock to the secluded island for family picnics. I was fortunate to have many visits to the island with my family growing up.

During his Green Island expedition, Lino spent time preparing in Massawa, which is only ten minutes away from the island by boat. Lino came into the Bazaar to collect some items and we began talking. Ever curious, I asked him what he was doing in Massawa and he came to life as he told me about his project. His eyes were sparkling and his hands were waving all over the place. I thought he would explode from the excitement!

He mentioned he was looking for young women to photograph so he could show off the scenery and asked if I would be interested. I said, "No". I was worried about not being photogenic. There were very few young women of my age in Massawa at the time, so he pleaded for me to reconsider. He told me he already had two other women lined up and they were coming in from other parts of Eritrea. The other two young women turned out to be a model from Asmara and Emma Bini, who went on to become French screen legend Philippe Leroy's third wife. I knew Emma's parents very well. They owned a high-end Italian Optometry business and they regularly holidayed as a family in Massawa. I came to meet Emma as they stayed next door to a very dear friends of mine, Antonio and Flora Vitanza. Emma was often quite aloof and we never really connected on a personal level.

Lino needed just one more model. I declined again, but he said he'd come back the next day to see if I had changed my mind.

I was speaking to a friend over a coffee later that afternoon and she chided me for refusing to help such a high profile person.

"What are you afraid of?" she asked.

"I am not afraid!" I shot back. "I just never thought I would be a model for such a high profile photographer and be in a magazine. What if I would be a disappointment to him?"

My friend was insistent. "People would throw themselves at this opportunity. Lino is world famous? Why would you miss out on this?" I knew she was right, so when he returned to the bazaar as promised, I had decided I would give it a go. "You only live once," I told myself.

We went over to Green Island by boat piloted by a

sailor that helped with the equipment. As soon as we were ashore, Lino managed to put me at ease, giving me instructions on how to pose and walk — to achieve what he wanted for his shoot. He photographed me in my swimming suit holding a swordfish nose with the skyline of Massawa in the background over the sea. In the next series of photos, I was in a sarong pretending to walk down the beach on Green Island. I felt like a superstar having my photo taken by an international journalist. Even though I never saw them run in the *Domenica Del Corriere*, the Italian weekly newspaper Lino worked for at the time.

Lino was kind enough to send me a couple of the photos he took, which I still have to this day. Although I felt puzzled about it all at the time, today I love those photos as they capture my youthful beauty and remind me of a time when I pushed myself outside of my comfort zone.

The Architecture of Massawa.

Ex Bank of Italy.

Torino Hotel.

Photos both pages
Courtesy of Piero Traversi

The Architecture of Massawa.

Ghebi, the Imperial Palace, Taulud.

Historical photo of centre of town.

Savoia Hotel.

LIVING ON THE PEARL OF THE RED SEA

The Architecture of Massawa.

Photos both pages by
Ghideon Musa Aron

Living on the Pearl of the Red Sea

The Architecture of Massawa.

LIVING ON THE PEARL OF THE RED SEA

The Architecture of Massawa.

Photos both pages by
Ghideon Musa Aron

The Architecture of Massawa.

LIVING ON THE PEARL OF THE RED SEA

The Architecture of Massawa.

Photos both pages by
Ghideon Musa Aron

LIVING ON THE PEARL OF THE RED SEA

The Architecture of Massawa.

LIVING ON THE PEARL OF THE RED SEA

The Architecture of Massawa.

Photos both pages by
Ghideon Musa Aron

LIVING ON THE PEARL OF THE RED SEA

The Architecture of Massawa.

LIVING ON THE PEARL OF THE RED SEA

The Architecture of Massawa.

Photos both pages by
Ghideon Musa Aron

Living on the Pearl of the Red Sea

The Architecture of Massawa.

LIVING ON THE PEARL OF THE RED SEA

The Architecture of Massawa.

Photos both pages by
Ghideon Musa Aron

LIVING ON THE PEARL OF THE RED SEA

The Architecture of Massawa.

LIVING ON THE PEARL OF THE RED SEA

The Architecture of Massawa.

Photos both pages by
Ghideon Musa Aron

LIVING ON THE PEARL OF THE RED SEA

The Architecture of Massawa.

Living on the Pearl of the Red Sea

The Architecture of Massawa.

Photos both pages by
Ghideon Musa Aron

LIVING ON THE PEARL OF THE RED SEA

The Architecture of Massawa.

Above and right: Sheik Seid Island, also known as Isola Verde.

Photo ©*Eufrasia Gagliardo*

Photos this page by *Ghideon Musa Aron*

The authors photo by Lino Pellegrini.

Photo ©Eufrasia Gagliardo

Camels of Massawa.

Photos this page by
Ghideon Musa Aron

Mary Cilia, the author's mother.

Photos both pages
©*Eufrasia Gagliardo*

Damiano Lucreziano, the author's father.

The author and her father, on the Asmara Cathedral stairs.

Photos both pages
©Eufrasia Gagliardo

The Gagliardo's stopover in Manila, Philippines, on their way to Australia. From left: Giampalo, Eufrasia, Mariangela, Luigi, Gianni.

The authors family. From left: Mother Mary, Father Damiano, the author and brother Paolo.

Ghergsum Beach.

Photos this page by
Ghideon Musa Aron

Ghergsum Beach.

The author, at back, and friends.

Photos this page
©*Eufrasia Gagliardo*

Yacht Club, Massawa.
The author and her cousin Rita Palmucci-Bonamego.

The Massawa Yacht Club pool.

*Navy Day Gala Dinner.
The author and Ethiopian & Italian Officers.*

Photos both pages
©Eufrasia Gagliardo

John Gagliardo - fishing trip to Dissei Island.

Photos both pages
©*Eufrasia Gagliardo*

John Gagliardo - fishing trip to Dissei Island.

Le Saline Di Massawa Salt Factory.

Photos both pages
Courtesy of Piero Traversi

Illustration by Aurora.

Aerial view of Taulud Island.

Massawa view.

Photos both pages by
Ghideon Musa Aron

Massawa view.

A Ghebena, a typical coffee maker.

Buon Respiro Ghinda. Suor Pia in centre.

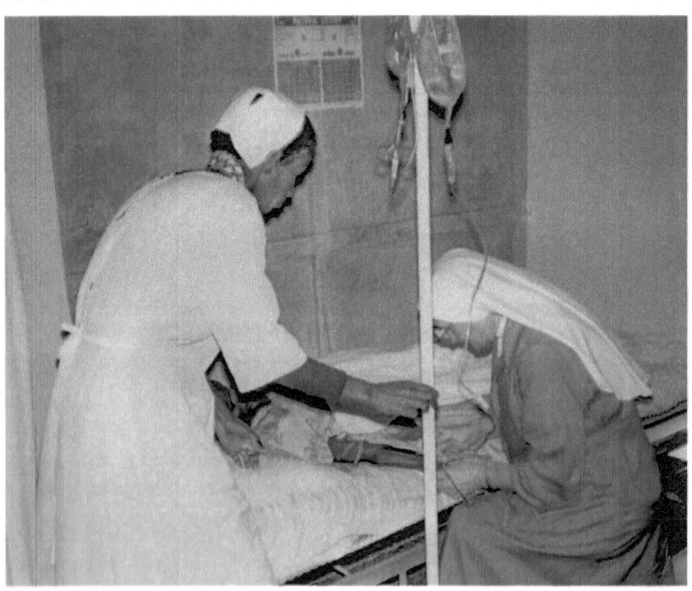

Suor Pia at her Asmara Clinic.

Suor Pia at Awassa with her orphans.

Photos both pages
©*Eufrasia Gagliardo*

LIVING ON THE PEARL OF THE RED SEA

Eritrean Orthodox Coptic Priests.

Eritrean Orthodox Coptic Priests.

Photos both pages by
Ghideon Musa Aron

The Israeli Fishermen

Whenever I Reminisce About my Early Life in Massawa, the ease of the way so many cultures were able to live together in harmony fills my heart with joy. In my experience, there was no racial discrimination and people made an effort to learn multiple languages so they would be able to communicate with anyone they met on the street.

Emperor Haile Selassie had given permission for Israeli finishing boats to frequent the Red Sea and harvest what they needed to take back to their homeland. It was common to see several Israeli fishing boats docked in a section of the port at Massawa as the crew rested in town. They were allocated their own space a distance away from the luxury yachts and tourist vessels so they could clean their nets, service their boats and store their fish without interrupting the bustling marina area.

I celebrated the Emperor's decision as many of the fishermen began to stop by the Bazaar for supplies and I came to know them well. I would ask them all kinds of questions about their homeland and became enamoured with their tales of the Biblical holy land and dreamed of visiting it one day.

I believe it is rare to find a Catholic person who doesn't wish to visit the holy land at least once in their lifetime. Even though I had completed all of my school years under the instruction of nuns and continued on to college at Santa Anna being immersed completely in my faith, I would still dream about la terra santa, the cradle of civilisation, and long to see the places where Jesus was born and raised and the locations where he performed his miracles. The idea of being able to follow in his footsteps many centuries later and pray where the Christian community was formed lit me up inside.

I had thought about it so much that I had even created an itinerary for myself. I would go to Nazareth, where God's angel visited the virgin Mary with the annunciation. To Bethlehem, the birthplace of Jesus, to see the Basilica della Natività. To Gethsemane, the garden across the Kidron Valley on the Mount of Olives, where Jesus was believed to have prayed before his arrest. To Jerusalem to visit the Church of the Holy Sepulchre, which includes two of the holiest Christian sites; the place where Jesus was crucified and the empty tomb, where he is believed to have been buried and resurrected. I used to get truly lost in this imaginative pilgrimage and I promised myself that I would do it one day.

The Emperor's decision to grant Israeli fishermen access to our waters made me feel like I was a step closer to realising my dream.

I came to befriend one of the captains and he would come to the Bazaar every time he was about to depart Massawa for a fishing trip or for the long journey back to Israel to sell the fruits of their latest expedition. On the few occasions he brought his wife with him, he would ask if she could contact me in his absence if she needed anything. Luckily such occasions never eventuated.

One day the captain offered for me to join them on a voyage to Israel. I was beyond excited and rushed home to ask my mother's permission to go. Her cheeks flushed a shade of beet red, and she declared, "No! No way! Are you crazy? This is not even up for discussion!"

For you see, it would be unheard of for an unmarried, single young woman to hop aboard a boat full of grown men to sail across the sea without a chaperone. It was not something I had thought about. For me, this was purely a holy experience.

Seeing my utter disappointment when I told the captain I couldn't go, he offered another solution. "I can let you know when my wife is next coming with us? It takes us fifteen days to arrive at Israel and fifteen days to come back. Because the crew each live in different parts of the country, like Bethlehem and Nazareth, we can ensure you have safe places to stay and it wouldn't cost you a cent."

The captain painted a picture that sounded absolutely divine. A free trip with lifts from one incredible town to the next, safe accommodation and the chance to explore the holy land.

"You have always been so welcoming to us here. We have arrived in a place where we don't know anybody, and you have shown us nothing but kindness. We know when we dock at Massawa, we have a friend here. Tell your mother you will be well looked after and you will have a woman with you at all times, you will never be a guest in a single man's house."

I felt buoyed by these terms and thought my mother might relax knowing they had already thought everything through for me. They were about to set out to Israel again and it would be a month before they returned. Their routine was to spend a month servicing their boats, fishing and then preparing to head off once again.

Despite this, my mother refused to budge. I tried several times to get her permission to go, but the answer remained the same. "Clear this from your mind, dear, it is never going to happen," she said. Even when I turned eighteen, I didn't dare to go without my mother's blessing.

Although I never did get to experience the trip I had dreamed of for many a night, the fishermen made a point of bringing me back small treasures from Israel. The fishermen I knew were not Catholic, but they knew religion was close to my heart and they would find ways to give me a taste of the country I could not visit.

On one trip, a crewman from Bethlehem bought me a rosary. On another, a crewmate from Jerusalem bought me back a small bottle filled with soil from a sacred site.

"If you can't go to Israel, Israel will come to you!" he declared proudly as he handed me the glass bottle, which I have kept among my prized possessions for decades since.

The *Journalist*

I was fortunate to meet many colourful characters in the eight years I managed the Bazaar. One of the men whom I had the great fortune of meeting was Ali Efendi. The young man wondered into my store with a spring in his step and a twinkle in his eye. Although he had a cheery disposition, it was impossible not to notice he had stumps where his forearms and hands should be.

I asked Ali many questions and quickly got to know him. He was friendly and very open in sharing how it was that he came to lose his arms. Ali was a lively and cheerful little boy that loved soccer. From the moment he could walk, he learned to kick a soccer ball and lived and breathed the sport. Ali had firm dreams of becoming an international football star and would be determined to make anything that was even remotely round into a makeshift soccer ball so he could practice his skills at every opportunity.

Ali was seven years old and was walking through a field when he spotted something that looked round enough to become his ball for the afternoon. He ran towards it and, puzzled by its texture, wondered whether it was some kind of exotic fruit. Well, it doesn't matter what it is, it's going to be my soccer ball, he thought as he picked it up with both hands.

He'd only been carrying the strange looking object for a matter of seconds before it exploded in his hands, sending a shock-wave of sound throughout the buildings surrounding the field. With memories of the carnage of World War II still fresh in the minds of many Massawa residents, the unexpected cacophony of sound polarised people. Some ran for their lives away from the field in utter terror, while others flocked to the field to uncover the mystery of its origin.

Those who were brave enough to venture onto the field found Ali, unconscious on the ground in a pool of his own blood with the majority of both forearms blown off. His hands were nowhere to be seen. Ali was rushed to the hospital and the team worked hard to save his life following so much trauma and blood loss.

Once the authorities investigated, they discovered Ali had picked up an undetonated live grenade. The simple act of him picking it up was enough to set off the device's countdown mechanism.

Although Ali never went into great detail with me about his recovery, one sentence he spoke with utter excitement has remained with me always, "I still have both my feet, so I can play soccer!" When he was well enough, Ali went back to school and began to master the use of his forearms in place of his once-nimble fingers. Prosthetics weren't readily accessible at the time, so the only way he could salvage any chance of an independent life was to learn how to work with his new arms.

He used his stumps to hold pens and could write. He could hold cutlery to feed himself and even learned how to ride a bicycle. There were many people who were forced to beg on the streets of Massawa in order to survive and he had seen amputees reduced to this form of existence. Ali knew he wasn't an invalid and he was determined to live life on his own terms.

So here he was, now a man several years my senior, standing inside the Bazaar, asking to speak to the manager… me. He had spent several minutes running his eyes over the covers of all of the newspapers and magazines we had in store. Meticulously reading every headline that screamed out from the pages in bold, black ink.

"Good afternoon signorina, I want to become a journalist. You have to help me," he said, with pleading eyes.

I had no idea how to respond. How am I supposed to help this man to become a journalist? I run a shop!

"A journalist? How can I help?"

"Yes, a journalist."

We weren't getting anywhere fast with this conversation, but there was something about this Muslim man and his sincerity that stopped me from walking away in frustration. Instead, I took a deep breath and tried again.

"How can I help you?" My persistence paid off. Ali indeed already had a plan and this was why he was standing in my shop. I was the only one who could help him to make his dream a reality.

"You can give me a loan so I can sell the Time magazines, the Newsweek and the newspapers. I know people are too busy to leave their offices each day to come here and buy it. I will be the journalist who brings them the news." Ali puffed his chest out and beamed with pride as he shared his business plan with me, but I needed to clarify something with him first....

"That's not what a journalist does! They write the stories that go into the newspapers, they don't sell the newspapers. Do you realise that?"

Unperturbed, Ali shrugged his shoulders and replied casually, "I don't care, I want to become a journalist."

I had to get clearance from the owner of the Bazaar to allow our newspaper delivery man, I mean, *journalist*, to begin his work. It was done so on the condition that if he never repaid his loan, it would come out of my pocket. I knew in my heart that Ali was genuine and wanted to make something of his life, so it was a condition I agreed to without hesitation – and without Ali knowing about it.

Ali began to build quite the business for himself. Each morning he would come into the Bazaar with a list of publications he wanted to collect for the day and he would set off, walking into every major office in town selling them to the business owners and their employees.

Ali quickly became an iconic symbol of resilience and determination on the island. Everyone could see that he could so easily have fallen into the life of a beggar, but through his positivity and bright spirit, he had created a job for himself. In the process, he had shown all of us that you can be or do anything you want... even become a *journalist* without formal qualifications!

Such was Ali's fame that Emperor Haile Selassie himself acknowledged Ali and gave him special permission to access the ports. Ali was the only person who was allowed on board every single cargo or military ship docking in Massawa to sell his wares to the crew. When it came to cruise ships, he would wait on the docks for the passengers to disembark so he could sell them newspapers and magazines.

Ali created the perfect lifestyle for himself, working by day and eating his fill at restaurants every night. I never asked him where he rested his head at night, but I think he must have had a place of his own as he was always so well presented in clean clothing and shined shoes. He never married, but the interactions he had with people of all walks of life every single day seemed to be all he needed to feel fulfilled.

From time to time, I would give him a friendly ribbing about continuing to call himself a journalist, but he stuck firmly to his title, introducing himself to those who met him for the first time as *Ali Efendi, the journalist*. As we got to know each other so well, he asked me how I was able to give him the loan and I told him the truth – I was vouching for him and his loan was my responsibility. He seemed taken aback by this at first, but I assured him I knew he was honest (aside from telling everyone he was a journalist!) and would pay it back when he could. This helped him to relax and we carried on with our usual routine.

Getting used to seeing his smiling face punctually around 9am every morning, a strangeness washed over me when he failed to show up for a few days in a row. With no way to contact Ali, I began to worry about him. My panic increased when a young man came into the Bazaar with a sombre expression and declared, "Ali sent me."

I bombarded him with questions.

"What's wrong with Ali? Is he hurt? Is he sick? I haven't seen him for a few days, is he okay?"

"He's sick. He thinks he's going to die."

My breath caught in my throat and I felt a dark energy begin to build in the pit of my stomach at the thought of Ali no longer being with us. He had become beloved by the whole town.

The man stepped forward and thrust his hand out and I saw it contained a roll of money.

"Ali doesn't want to die if he hasn't paid off his loan to you. He wanted to pay what he owes so he can die in peace."

I fought back tears as I accepted the money.

"Okay...." It was all I could manage.

The man left as quickly as he had arrived and I was left there, all alone, holding the roll of notes.

Oh my God!

As fate would have it, the illness wasn't enough to kill Ali and he came back to visit me a few weeks later to resume his *journalist* duties, this time as a fully self-funded businessman.

Ali is one of those incredible human beings who changes you and makes you a better person simply for knowing them. Despite his potentially crippling handicap in those times, Ali Efendi went back to school and went on to build a business and a life for himself.

He never did become an internationally famous soccer player, instead he became a *journalist* and cemented himself as a Massawan icon.

THE OYSTER MAN

MASSAWA WAS KNOWN FONDLY AROUND the world as *The Pearl of the Red Sea*. The depths of the azure water that surrounded the island kept a plethora of pearl-laden oysters safe. They came in so many varieties from pure white and cream to black and pink. Many a diver made their fortunes from harvesting oysters from the sea and the one I had the greatest interaction with was a man by the name of Hashabella.

What made Hashabella different from the many other pearl-seekers is he lived a very simple life. While others in the industry enjoyed a high life of luxury, Hashabella owned a very modest hut with only the bare essentials; a bed lined with straw that rested on the floor, a charcoal stove that had the dual purpose of heating the house as well as being the only way he could cook his meals. The white walls were bare, with the exception of a few homemade shelves constructed with wood offcuts that were lined with jam jars he collected.

The only possession of note, which took pride of place in the centre of his hut, was an ornate multi-coloured plate with stunning emerald hues. The presence of such a luxury in what was otherwise a very basic home was not too out of the ordinary – many African and Arabic families have at least one plate such as this.

Every morning, before the sun would rise above the sea, Hashabella would leave his home and untie his small dingy from its usual position on the jetty. Without the aid of an engine, a GPS or a map, he would row out to a very specific spot where he knew a prosperous oyster colony thrived. He guarded that spot with his life, never writing down anything and relying solely on his memory and his nautical navigation skills to be able to pinpoint the location in order to return without fail every single day.

He would work quickly and effortlessly, harvesting the day's quota of oysters and adding them to his straw satchel bag. Pearlers at the time were predominantly Somalian and Arabic and they were extremely skilled at navigating the task. The only equipment they needed was a clamp to close their nostrils, a heavy stone to weigh them down to the sea floor and a skill for working efficiently. On each breath, Hashabella would drop down, fill his straw bag with as many shells as he could reach and then resurface when he needed a breath. Many seasoned free divers could manage intervals varying between one and three minutes. The trade-off was they often didn't venture into depths greater than 18 to 20 metres, leaving a lot of the deeper oyster clusters untouched.

Once he'd cleaned his tools, Hashabella would row to the Yacht Club where he knew he would find a captive clientele who also had an insatiable appetite for fresh oysters. Having an amicable relationship with the owner of the venue helped him immensely and Hashabella was given free rein to approach club members to offer them his wares.

At midday, as sharp as a Swiss clock, his tall, lean figure would appear on the deck of the Yacht Club smelling like the sea with a broad, toothless smile and his straw bag full of juicy oysters. He wore an old panama hat and a fabric sash around his hips that did little to disguise his sun-bleached and worn out boardshorts.

As someone who followed the island tradition of closing the Bazaar at midday to enjoy some drinks and the chance to play table tennis or a game of cards with friends and family, I often found myself at the Yacht Club – the Massawa hot spot – to have an aperitif and wait for Hashabella's arrival. We had a tradition of rolling some dice to determine who would pay for the next round of drinks – the person who rolled the lowest number copped the bill – and it was quite common for the dice to end up in the pool! Of course, whoever lost the dice would automatically pay.

Even those who had brought their swimmers along to enjoy a refreshing swim in the natural pool at the Yacht Club would rush to grab their towels and find a table when Hashabella arrived. Even the captivating environment filled with a kaleidoscope of corals, anemones, seashells and marine life could not keep them from the involuntary rumble in their stomachs that happened whenever midday struck.

He wasted little time and from the moment he stepped onto the deck, he would begin his rounds, approaching every single table and he found very little resistance to his proposition. Most people would already have ordered a cold drink and were simply waiting for Hashabella's succulent and juicy oysters.

Nimble with his hands and having perfected the art of opening the oysters and shucking them with ease, Hashabella was somewhat of an unintentional showman as people marvelled at the way he swiftly served up their oysters with a squeeze of lime before moving on to the next table. There was, however, one condition to buying from Hashabella – he would never sell you less than a dozen oysters at a time.

"You can't have one! More is better!" he would exclaim. "I'll give you a dozen."

He was an incredible salesman and because he was a fixture of the town and so pleasant with everyone, he got away with it every single time.

Being an observant person, I noticed that there would be

occasions when Hashabella would open up an oyster and quickly discharge it back into his straw bag. The occasion came when he did this when he got to my table, so I asked him what was wrong with the oyster.

"Ah! It's not fresh... not fresh...." he muttered in response as he reached for another oyster to serve to me. If you have only just been diving, and walked straight in here from the sea, how can it not be fresh? I puzzled quietly. But I didn't press him any further on it. I was fond of him, just like everyone else in town, and I didn't want to hurt his feelings by questioning him in that moment.

I had my suspicions about what was going on, but it bothered me that I didn't know for sure. So on another occasion, I struck up a conversation with Hashabella as he began to serve up another dozen of his delectable morsels for me and my friends. I simply couldn't resist! I asked him if he ever found pearls in the oysters and if he had ever considered becoming a pearl merchant. It was apparent in his physical appearance and the way he lived so simply that he wasn't flush with money despite the potential.

Working in the Bazaar and interacting with people from many different countries, I was fluent in Italian, Arabic and English. I knew Hashabella was Arabic, so I spoke to him in his native language.

"You could sell them for a handsome price and live a very different life if you wanted to. What do you do with all the pearls that you find?"

Hashabella's face relaxed and he stopped what he was doing as he eyes took on a dream-like quality.

"When I have enough pearls, I will sell them all," he said.

"Then what? What are you going to do with all that money?" I asked, satisfied that I now knew he was quickly throwing pearl-laden oysters back into his bag before we, his customers, could see what was inside.

"I'm going to move to Naples where I will live the life of a lord."

His dream was not what I expected, and I wanted to ask him more about how he came to learn of Naples and decide it was his dream destination. He may have heard tales from Italian travellers about the southern seaside city and fallen in love with the idea that he could one day retire there and enjoy the fruits of many years of hard work.

This conversation started up a great friendship and every time I was at the Yacht Club when Hashabella arrived, I would ask him how he was and whether he'd had any encounters with sharks that day. He always took the time to converse and these exchanges became a highlight for both of us.

He described his home and daily life to me and said the jam jars he found discarded around Massawa were washed and became his basic pearl safes. He would store his finds in them and keep them on the shelves in his hut. With no security, it was a marvel he was able to do this for years on end without being subjected to a robbery.

One day, Hashabella was shucking oysters for me as we chatted and he paused suddenly as he opened the oyster. I continued talking, oblivious to his sudden halt because he recovered quickly and added a squeeze of lime onto the oyster before passing it to me. Without hesitation, I lifted the shell to my lips and slid the morsel into my mouth. Now, it is important that I share that I was never one to simply gulp an oyster down in one go, it never felt nice to me. So I would take the time to chew it and enjoy the taste before swallowing it like I would any other food.

On this occasion, I felt a distinct crunch as I bit down on the oyster – something I had never experienced before from one of Hashabella's oysters. Trying so hard to appear like everything was okay so as not to hurt his feelings, I continued to chew a little more delicately before swallowing. There must have been a bit of loose shell in that one, I told myself.

But Hashabella was staring at me, with a furrowed brow as I proceeded to eat the oyster. Oh gosh! He knows he's given me a bad oyster! I smiled widely as soon as I swallowed to try to cover it up, but Hashabella's expression was indecipherable. I couldn't tell if he was upset or angry, but I didn't have to wait long to find out.

"Are you stupid?" he said in a hushed tone so as not to cause a scene. "You just ate a pearl!"

He didn't keep the pearl for himself! Panic set in as I realised the gravity of what had just happened. Hashabella had decided our friendship was such that he would give up one of his pearls – one of his tickets to Naples and realising his dream – to surprise me with a gift. And I had eaten it.

I apologised profusely and felt absolutely terrible that I had robbed him of the chance to surprise me with something beautiful and unexpected, but Hashabella quickly saw the funny side of it all and joked that only someone like me would eat a pearl and think nothing of it.

Our friendship continued for many years, until I left Massawa in 1971. I'll never know if Hashabella was able to make his dream a reality, although I wish with all of my heart he did. One thing I do know for sure is he never tried to surprise me with a pearl ever again.

The Young Bride and the Black Pearl

T̲he Golden Bachelor of Massawa in the 1960s was the general practitioner, Dr Michelangelo Trimarchi. He was wealthy and had the prestigious position of working as the head of the Massawa Hospital as well as having his own private clinic. He had the physique of a sportsman and a head of hair complemented by a thin, black moustache that gave him an uncanny resemblance to American film icon Clarke Gable.

He had a strut and held his head up high, staring the world boldly in the face whenever he walked around town. To me, his presence shouted, "I am proud of who I am, feel free to look at me."

Michelangelo knew every woman in the town had a crush on him and knew whenever he took his impressive yacht out for a sail, he would capture the attention of every female, single or married, on the shoreline. They would marvel at him as he released the sails and alighted up the mast with the prowess of a professional athlete. On other days, he would swim laps in the natural pool at the Yacht Club, much to the delight of the female members there at the time.

While Michelangelo's medical accomplishments as a GP and surgeon were beyond reproach, he was also renowned for his sailing achievements. He was a local champion and would spend countless hours priming his yacht for competitions, which he embarked on with a seasoned and loyal crew. They were determined to win every race they entered and he became a multi-award winning champion, creating almost unbeatable competition for anyone else who entered his categories.

The sailing regattas were held in the same high regard as the America's Cup and the prestige of being a champion opened boundless doors for Michelangelo and despite his busy schedule, he always supported the *Miss Barca a vela* (Miss Sailing Boat) pageant, which was held at the Yacht Club after the racing was over.

The election of *Miss Barca a vela* was a real event, all of the young teenage women would enter and be anxious to see who would be crowned, a challenge of who had the best evening dress. Their admirers had to vote for the ladies, then there was the coronation.

Despite the possibility of being swept away with all the

adoration heaped upon him, Michelangelo kept his feet firmly planted on the ground. He was far from stuck-up despite his wealth, local fame and all of the trappings that went with it.

While he never had to work hard to attract the attention of women, his head was very rarely turned until Giulia Ferraciolo moved to town. They connected on the tennis court – the only one in Massawa that was nestled across the canal right next to the petrol refinery. With a shared love of the sport, they quickly bonded.

Giulia came from a very wealthy family and had moved to Massawa following the breakdown of her first marriage. She was young, beautiful and also an intellectual match, having a university degree of her own. By all accounts, she was the perfect bride and it didn't take Michelangelo long to recognise that.

After a short courtship, they were married in a magnificent wedding. As this was her second marriage, Giulia followed the tradition of avoiding a white dress and instead chose an off-white Chanel dress with a matching jacket and voluminous iconic Chanel hat. Michelangelo looked dashing in an off-white Panama suit with a bow tie instead of his usual slim-line neck tie. The exclusive affair was attended by all of Massawa's VIPs, and they sweltered through the ceremony on what turned out to be a forty-five degree day.

Refreshments were abundant at the CIAAO Hotel, the

luxury setting of their wedding reception, in an attempt to cool guests and the new bride and groom down. CIAAO, the same hotel I used to marvel at from the windows in my childhood home, was the destination for all the high profile visitors to Massawa, from celebrity actors and actresses through to international royalty.

Once the formalities were over, the newly-weds wasted no time escaping to Nairobi, the capital of Kenya. Back then, it was the première destination for wealthy couples to honeymoon as they could go on safari and admire the country's majestic wildlife. The more adventurous could climb Mount Kilimanjaro and those who were less adventurous could choose from the many resorts to relax poolside. Literary fans could also experience the Serengeti and other locations brought to life in Ernest Hemingway's books. Nairobi definitely had plenty going for it.

Once the honeymoon was complete, the couple came back to Massawa rested and relaxed and settled into Michelangelo's home. Typical of Massawan architecture, his home was an all-white two-storey home with verandas wrapping around both levels. Inside, the high ceilings maximised the sea breezes to try to stave off the oppressive heat of the midday sun and every room was adorned with luxurious furniture.

The surrounding tropical gardens were filled with palms to cast small pools of shade on the manicured lawns and splashes of colour were provided by the pink oleander blooms, white frangipani and vibrant oranges and purples from the bougainvillea. Their scents provided a beautiful perfume around the home.

The house was fully staffed, with a team of servants who would cater to every whim of the new Mr and Mrs Trimarchi as well as any of the guests. When they decided to have an intimate party, free from the pomp and ceremony that was their official wedding, my mother was lucky enough to be invited to their home for the occasion.

My mother was the best friend of Giulia's mother and Giulia would come to my mother often to have her dreams interpreted. When my mother came home, she told me those who were invited in were greeted at the door by a finely dressed maid carrying a silver platter of crystal glasses filled with ice-cold fresh lemonade.

It is an Italian tradition to display all of the gifts given to the couple for their wedding. The tables of elegantly-wrapped gifts were displayed at their public wedding, but the couple had been in such a rush to start their honeymoon, they had not opened any of their gifts before they left for Nairobi. To ensure the tradition was respected, their gifts were brought home by their staff and rearranged in another luxurious display guests at their private gathering could admire.

It would have been a real challenge to buy a gift for a couple who already had everything they could ever desire. My mother told me how they unwrapped gifts of silver, gold, crystal and even a coffee set made from the finest and most precious English porcelain. It was the latter that caught my mother's attention. The set was painted with intricate floral designs and included a milk jar, sugar bowl, side plates for cakes and other high tea essentials.

The gift came from a wealthy Yemenite pearl dealer who wore kaftans in all sorts of luxurious materials and colours often accompanied with an embroidered white jacket. I never saw him wear a suit. The businessman would export Red Sea Pearls his divers extracted from the Dahlak Islands and he was unafraid of exhibiting his unimaginable wealth.

Guests marvelled at the gift, but it wasn't until everyone went home and Giulia went to put away the porcelain set that she discovered something out of the ordinary. There was a small black silk bag tucked into the lid of the sugar bowl. Intrigued, she pulled it out and opened the frayed drawstring to see what was hidden inside.

She gasped in horror as she saw it was filled with several little black balls. Black magic! Despite her high intellect, her mind immediately leapt to this conclusion and panic set in. Giulia believed the businessman must have used the gift as a secret means of cursing her and her marriage.

It was common knowledge in Massawa that you could, if you chose to, visit certain individuals on the island and they would give you the means through which you could cast a bad spell, *fattura*, on someone.

As I shared in the lady of the spells chapter, this was the

culture of the Eritreans and it didn't mean much to me, but some Italians who had come to live on the island believed this was possible with all of their heart. Clearly, Giulia was one of those people.

With fear causing her hands to tremble, Giulia ran to the bathroom and threw the little black balls into the toilet and flushed them down. Pushing the buttons several times to make sure they were gone for good, she retreated back to her bed to lie down until her body stopped shaking and she caught her breath back.

Months went by and the couple were enjoying life locked in their wedded bliss and one day, the businessman turned up at Michelangelo's clinic feeling unwell. The doctor checked him over and once he had finished the consultation, the conversation became more personal in nature. The businessman was anxious to know if they had found his little extra gift as he had not heard anything from the couple since their private party.

No longer worried about it being a surprise, the businessman asked outright, "Did your new wife love the surprise I hid in the sugar bowl?"

What surprise? the doctor thought.

"I put 20 black pearls in there for her, so she could make them into some nice jewellery to wear on evenings out," the businessman revealed.

"Oh! Thank you so much for your generosity!"

When the doctor returned home to his bride that evening,

he shared the revelation and urged her to go and check the sugar bowl in the cupboard. Giulia turned white and her eyes widened in horror as she realised what she had done – flushed away thousands of dollars' worth of black pearls that fateful day when she mistook them for being the work of a witchdoctor or voodoo practitioner.

The Button Man

Whenever You Set Foot on the Shore of Massawa for the first time, your nostrils are assaulted with the acrid smell of rotting shellfish. It is everywhere on the breeze and if you spend any amount of time along the beach, like I did, you would go home with the stench clinging to your clothes and your hair. I didn't mind the smell, it smelt of home. For visitors, it did take a bit of getting used to.

For regulars, feeling the familiar sting as your brain registers the smells, forcing tears to prick the corners of your eyes, you knew you had almost reached your destination. You would smell the island long before you could sneak a glimpse of it along the winding roads that led to the floating bridge. It was a welcome relief for those who may have driven for two hours from Asmara.

Being someone who was prone to carsickness, the roads in and out of Massawa were a nightmare for me, so being able to smell the seashells was a relief in more ways than one. The culprit were trochus shells. Their conic shape, adorned with pink and white raised nodules, looked like intricate lace-work from a distance. As a child, I turned empty trochus shells upside down in my hand and pretended they were ice cream cones.

Although the outside of the shells are beautiful, it was what was inside them that created a burgeoning industry for Massawa – mother of pearl.

Being a mollusc, trochus is abundant in mother of pearl, which lined the inside of the sturdy shells. The iridescent lining that has been used for centuries by many different cultures around the world for jewellery, home decorations and even to adorn the hilts of weapons, is created by nacre. This is a protection mechanism of the living mollusc and whenever something foreign enters its shell, the snail will coat it in nacre to protect itself. Residual nacre sits inside the shell and when the snail moves on or perishes, the shell can be re-purposed in dozens of useful ways.

The iridescent shells are called mother of pearl because nacre is the same substance that is used to create pearl gemstones. In oysters, when a grain of sand gets inside the shell, the organism inside will coat the grain of sand with layer upon layer of nacre, creating the round pearl three or four years later. Therefore, the shells, with their nacre lining, are the from which pearls are *born*.

This story is about Signor Giordano, the man who used mother of pearl to create a successful international button business. He was a big thinker and an innovator, importing production machinery from Italy that was the first of its kind at the time in order to produce the buttons on mass from Massawa. He employed Eritreans from all walks of life and his factory was highly respected.

He had divers who would gather the shells, sambuki owners who could load the shells aboard their vessels and transport them back to the shore where they would be piled into small mountains to dry out. This is what created the unique scent of the Massawa shoreline.

When the shells are ready, they were transported to the factory for processing. From there, Signor Giordano had a team of staff whose sole job was to select the biggest, most beautiful shells that would produce the largest pieces of mother of pearl. These were then taken to the craftspeople, whose job it was to take the raw shell and carry out the delicate work of transforming them into ornate buttons. This involved removing the external, hard shell – the lace-work as I call it – leaving behind the pure mother of pearl that could then be worked with.

The mother of pearl would be cut into strips, which could be used as jewellery or in home décor tiles, and the rest would be further refined into buttons in all shapes and sizes from traditional round to elegant flower designs and anything else you could imagine. This was done by the skilled hands of the craftspeople who manned the Tornio

– a machine for shaping which turns the piece of mother of pearl against a tool held steady by the operator.

Once the buttons were made, they would be lovingly packed by a group of women and prepared for shipment to their final destination. The journey of each of the buttons was far from over, however, as they could land on the desk of designers for Valentino, who declared mother of pearl was an elite adornment for his clothing and the humble Massawan shells would go on to feature on haute couture fashion pieces. They could be fixed to the shirt of a white collar worker in America or even onto the smocks of the Massawan school children.

While impressed by the first two, it was the last revelation that Signor Giordano shared with the dozens of students who toured his factory for field trips each year that made their eyes go as wide as saucers. The fact that their buttons had once been the shells of snail that lives under the sea made the students excited and daydreaming about the adventures their buttons must have been on. Until then, they had never given a second thought to the buttons down the back of their white smocks they had to fiddle with each and every day before and after school.

The youngsters under grade eight would wear white smocks with blue ribbons for boys and pink for the girls. From grade eight through to graduation, the smocks were black. After leaving the factory, every student had a new level of appreciation for something as previously boring as a button.

"Is that for real?" the children would exclaim.

Signor Giordano always loved field trip days and proudly shared more with the children, enjoying the pure delight and wonder in their eyes.

"My buttons are going all over the world and could be worn by anyone," he said with a wink, sending their imaginations into overdrive.

"You mean, the Pope would wear buttons that come from here?" enquired one child.

"What about Kings and Queens?" another chimed in.

"I presume so...." Signor Giordano would reply with a kind smile.

At this, the children would be struck dumb and stare around the factory in amazement. Before they left the factory, Signor Giordano would give each child a couple of mother of pearl buttons to take home with them and they treasured them as if they were made of gold. With a couple of buttons jingling in their hot little pockets, they couldn't wait to get home to show off their new prized possessions to their parents.

These were the days long before mass produced plastic became a major competitor for hand-crafted mother of pearl buttons, and I always smile when I think of what Signor Giordano was able to achieve. His humble Massawa factory supplied buttons to an international market while also providing so many jobs for people.

The Aquarium Filler

Tourists were commonplace in Massawa, with people flocking to the pristine shores from all around the world. But I knew there was something different about Luciano when I first met him.

With light brown hair in a mass of curls and a strong physique, Luciano was a handsome man, but his eyes... they were large, round and dark brown, lined with the longest lashes I had ever seen. His eyes made me think of Bambi and I was incredibly jealous that a man had been blessed with such eyelashes.

Luciano was born in a beautiful and renowned city in Northern Italy called Torino. Torino is an important business and cultural centre in Italy and is also known for its refined architecture, cuisine and beautiful mountainous areas – the Alps.

Luciano however loved the ocean and the warm climates. He visited regularly from Turin with friends, who were a couple. Comparatively speaking, the North Italian city was a very cold place. King Victor Emmanuel II, who became the first king of a united Italy in 1861, was born there. Luciano and his friends seemed to revel in being able to soak up the humidity and the reliable sunshine whenever they visited Massawa.

I crossed paths with them as the holiday apartment they regularly rented was next to my friend's house and I would see them heading off to the beach carrying diving equipment. They were affluent people, able to rent the same apartment regularly, hire a boat and spend countless hours exploring the marine life just off the coast of Massawa and all the way out to the Dahlak islands.

Over time, we became friends and Luciano asked if we could stay in touch while he was back home in Turin. "Would you give me your address so I can write to you?" he asked.

"Just put my name on the postcard and *Massawa* as the address and it will get to me!" I replied. The population was small enough that the post officer knew long term residents by name. I received a letter from him one year later, telling me about his life and asking questions about what it was like to live on the island and if it was safe.

When he graduated from secondary school with a degree in surveying it was time for him to choose his future path.

The thought of him being enclosed in an office or on a site didn't appeal to him, it just didn't fill him with passion. So he decided that he needed to follow his heart and find his place in the world and preferably near the sea. Luciano loved coming to Massawa and he felt at home there, so he researched his options and being a free spirit too he choose to leave his city life in Italy and move to Massawa. He came to Massawa with a plan in mind of how he would bring his passion to life and bring a little bit of the ocean he loved so much into everyone's home.

One day he walked into the Bazaar with a big smile on his face. I had to do a double-take to make sure it was really him. Once I registered it was him, I shook my head and started laughing.

"Why are you laughing?" he asked, with the smile refusing to budge from his face as his Bambi eyes twinkled.

"Because I think you're mad, leaving Italy to come back here!"

He refused to believe that, saying it was something his heart had wanted for a long time and he had finally built up enough courage to follow his dream. Turning to business, he asked if he could subscribe to Turin's newspaper, *La Stampa*, so he could keep on top of everything that was happening in his hometown.

I asked about his friends and they preferred to stay in Turino. I was his only friend on the island and was happy when he rented the same apartment close to my friend's place, so he was nearby. The apartment was massive, taking up one side of the multi-storey building.

Being an attractive single man, he quickly caught the attention of the young women who came to Massawa during the holidays. They were completely intrigued by him. But Luciano was too busy building his new life, which revolved around daily fishing trips, collecting his weekly La Stampa magazine and then visiting the post office to collect his mail. Occasionally he would meet with me for friendly conversations over coffee.

Knowing I was happily dating Gianni *John* Gagliardo at the time, my girlfriends would constantly bug me about Luciano, wanting to know if I could connect them to him as he never showed any interest whatsoever in talking to them. His life revolved around the fish he was catching and building his lucrative business of exporting unique species of Massawan fish to the international market. There was a healthy demand from wealthy people with majestic private aquariums seeking exotic fish for their collections and Luciano provided a means for them to acquire what they wanted.

"Why is he such a hermit? Why won't he go out? Why doesn't he have a girlfriend?"

I had to field all of these questions and more from my female friends because they continued to come up against a brick wall whenever they tried to engage with Luciano on his very rare public outings. Whenever I expressed my frustrations to him about constantly being hounded by these women, Luciano laughed it off and said he was happy with things the way they were.

Soon, I began to notice some jealousy creeping into the tones of some of my female friends, who came to Massawa for their holidays.

"You are the only one he talks to. You are the only one who goes to his house. Could you please organise a way for us to meet him?"

With this continuing week after week, I snapped and said to Luciano one day, "Listen, you have to get these ladies off my back. They are accusing me of being possessive of you, they believe I have some sort of grip on you when I really don't and it needs to stop. You need to stop hiding from them! Can you let me invite some of these women who are so madly in love with you and we can all get together?"

Seeing how much it was affecting me, Luciano reluctantly agreed and a small group of women were aflutter at the chance to finally get some face time with their mystery man. When we got together, I would invite some friends along and we would all talk about movies, books and art. While I know Luciano did enjoy the social interaction, he seemed oblivious to the fact that all of these women were after him.

Luciano went on to buy some land in the city right next to the church and built a home and an enormous shed that became the base for his business. He couldn't have chosen a site with a better outlook if he had tried. His view included Green Island, which was off the coast directly in front of him, and behind that towered Mount Ghedem. Luciano could sit on the veranda and simply enjoy the scenery. If you looked out to the right hand side, there was a causeway with the full view of Massawa City, the port and the railway.

At night time, the view was even more incredible. The Port was swarming with activity, glittering lights and sounds. You could see the ships entering the port and being guided by the pilot boats. There were ship sailing away and cranes that were loading and unloading vessels of all the cargo. There were voices echoing in the night with instructions and directions only matched by the sound of the trains arriving and leaving port. The nocturnal life of the port was something to experience, and Luciano had a front row seat to it all.

He was almost single-minded in his focus and it was firmly on improving his business and creating a bigger reach for exporting his fish. Luciano fitted out his shed with top of the line tanks and filtering equipment so he could house any of the 1000 species of fish and 220 species of coral found in the Red Sea off Massawa.

He was sending little pieces of paradise from the island that had quickly become his home to clients all over the world. The whole thing was funny for me, I had never thought about having a home aquarium because from the moment I was old enough to swim, I had been spending time with the sea life that thrived right on my doorstep. It made me feel grateful that I didn't have to spend so much money to have them shipped in to be able to appreciate their beauty.

As his business grew, Luciano bought a couple of sambuki and began to employ divers to head out to collect the fish and he employed people to manage his transition aquariums until the orders came through. This freed Luciano up to be able to pick and choose which expeditions he went on and to pursue some of the rarer species of fish that could be more difficult to locate.

By the time John and I left Massawa, Luciano's business had reached the point where fish would be transported to Asmara on a weekly basis and then flown to Bologna in Italy, where they would go on to their new homes elsewhere in the world.

When we came back to Massawa in 1975 for a visit, I reconnected with Luciano and went to visit him at his thriving business. We had Luigi and Mariangela with us and Luciano spent an hour taking them on a private tour of his business. He delighted at seeing them so intrigued by his aquariums and told them all about the different varieties of fish and what made them so special.

"You mean, they will go to live with important people around the world?" Luigi and Mariangela asked in wonder.

"Yes! Whoever wants to have one for their aquarium will have the fish I send to them," Luciano responded, his

Bambi eyes twinkling as he watched the children's mouths drop open in awe.

While the children were doing their second walk through the shed, I asked how Luciano had been, enquiring if he had a girlfriend or wife to keep him from living and breathing only his business. He looked down at me with a serious face and said, "No Eufrasia, I am gay."

Suddenly those years of having girls chase him with no reciprocation made perfect sense to me. I lost contact with Luciano after that visit, so I do not know if he was ever able to find love. But I do know his passion for his work remained as strong as ever.

The Kon Tiki

Luxury Yachts of all Shapes and Sizes Made their way into the port of Massawa laden with wealthy people from all around the world looking to experience the magic of the island. But none of them compare with the Kon Tiki. This super-yacht appeared offshore in the marina as if out of nowhere one fine day. It was too large to dock in the usual positions and the town was abuzz with excitement about who it could belong to.

"It must be someone super famous," they chattered.

"I wonder if it is a billionaire?"

"Why didn't they dock at the yacht club like everyone else?"

It turned out I didn't have to wait long to get a direct answer to the questions. The captain of the Kon Tiki walked through the doors of the Bazaar. After my polite round of questioning as he perused the shelves, I came to learn the Kon Tiki was owned by a group of millionaire Italian businessmen. They usually holidayed in the Maldives or Madagascar, but had been captivated by Massawa after learning of its beautiful underwater landscape, which I believe is second only to Australia's Great Barrier Reef.

As experienced divers and fishermen, they wanted to spend time in Massawa and venture off to the nearby Dahlak islands. The Dahlak Islands are actually an archipelago in the Red Sea – a collection of two large and 124 small islands. They are renowned as having an abundance of pearls and with only four of the islands containing permanent residents, the rest of the archipelago is ripe for exploration both above and below the water.

At certain times of the year, the islands become a resting stop for flamingos and their flurry of pick-tinged wings are the icing on the cake for what is a natural paradise. The sea surrounding the islands changes seamlessly from a midnight blue to a sparkling turquoise as you get closer to the shore. The dark pockets you can see from the surface indicate there are reefs below the water, a stark contrast to the bursts of colour divers find when they explore the sea depths. Like Green Island, a plethora of wild rock formations have been created inland on many of the Dahlak islands, giving each one a unique personality and energy. The whole package is absolutely to die for.

On the few inhabited islands, passers-by marvel at the simplicity of the small huts perched around the somewhat harsh landscape. Most tourists access the islands aboard sambuk boats and take their own camping equipment if they wish to stay overnight. But with the Kon Tiki at their disposal, these high flying corporate people were in the 1% category and would be able to access any areas they wished to without worry of where to rest their heads that night.

I found it amusing to learn that the Kon Tiki had arrived without its guests on board. They did not want to waste any time travelling on the sea, so they instead arrived on a private plane a day or two later. The captain had been given permission to allow residents to go on board the impressive vessel to explore it before the businessmen arrived for their holiday. The town was abuzz with excitement as those who made the most of the opportunity arrived back with reports of how the Kon Tiki was equipped with the latest and greatest fishing gear, jet skis, water skiing equipment and even its own shark cage as one of the businessmen was keen to dive in known shark territory between the islands. All of this was on top of the elite furnishings, luxury fittings and spacious areas. They had virtually created a palace on the sea.

Even though they had the ability to sleep on board for their entire trip, the men would only venture out for a couple of days at a time before returning to the Hotel Savoia in Massawa, where they had booked out all of the top-end rooms. I could see the hotel from my work and watched as they left to head out to the Kon Tiki on their next adventure. It seemed like a very charmed life and I was always curious about what they would be getting up to.

Once again, I didn't have to wait too long to find out. Signora Teresa connected with the group pretty early on and she invited me to a few afternoon teas with all of them. We would sit down at the Café Savoia with cappuccinos and I would be free to satisfy my curiosity by getting to know them. Most of the them worked for a chemical industry giant and others were in building, construction and fashion. One was even a Countess.

Of all of them, I came to know a young man by the name of Alberto the best. He was a handsome man with a friendly nature, but he seemed a little more untamed than the rest of the group. He had piercing green eyes and long blonde hair that he often wore loose around his shoulders. The rest of the businessmen had wives or girlfriends back home and Alberto seemed to be the only bachelor among them.

On their first trip out on the sea, Alberto managed to break his ankle while water skiing, so he couldn't join the rest of the group on the Kon Tiki for the remainder of the trip. He was really upset by this, but when he learned that I would be at the Bazaar working every day, he started to hobble across the road to visit with me each morning.

I could tell he was desperate to break the monotony of his days now that he was injured and one day, he noticed my bicycle parked to the side of the Bazaar.

"Is that yours?" he asked, pointing to the bicycle.

"Uh, yeah," I replied.

"Can I borrow it?"

"What for? You are injured!"

"I cannot walk far, but I'd get around much further if I had a bicycle. I'm sure I'd be able to ride it," he said, puffing out his chest slightly, maybe to appear more capable than what I thought he was.

I saw the pleading in his eyes and couldn't say no to him.

"You must promise me you will be careful, I don't want to be responsible if you have an accident in this madness."

A smile immediately spread across his face and he thanked me profusely.

The next morning, he started a routine of arriving to visit me at the Bazaar and then taking my bike to ride around the island. When he came back, he would fill me in on his day's adventures and I could see how much he enjoyed feeling like part of the environment there. I noticed his clothing begin to transform from the high-end designer threads he brought with him to the much more casual kaftans the locals wore. He would mingle with residents, spending time in the Arabic quarter drinking coffee in the markets and hang out on the shore with the local fishermen and others who made their livelihood from the sea.

As the days went on, he ventured further and further afield, and my anxiety went through the roof. I was so busy in the Bazaar that I did not have the time to keep track of him.

"Please Alberto, be safe. I don't want to be responsible for you now that I've given you the means to ride around the place."

He chuckled at my concern and I was thankful that I never had to go and rescue him off the side of the road following an accident. He returned my bike safely every afternoon without fail.

When the rest of the businessmen returned from the Dahlak islands, they extended an invitation through Signora Teresa for me to join them aboard Kon Tiki for a farewell dinner. I told her I wasn't interested, because the moment they left Massawa, I would likely not see them ever again.

"Alberto has been talking so much about you, they would like to meet you. Why don't you just join us?" she urged, almost exasperated that I didn't simply join her as I usually would. Teresa knew there were no other young women of my age around at that time. They were either much younger or older and already married. She believed there was no harm in entertaining a possible match with Alberto. In some respects, I was the most eligible bachelorette in Massawa! But I didn't want a bar of any of it. I could have gone to meet with Alberto and started a romance – any self-respecting gold digger would have – but that simply was not me. I didn't care for riches, wealth and power.

Not only that, but I had spent most of the time we'd known each other panicking that he was going to hurt himself even more on his crazy adventures around the island, riding a bike with a broken ankle. I was worried about the behaviour of someone who was more than ten years my senior! That is not the best foundations on which to lay a potential relationship.

I eventually agreed to join Teresa for the dinner and we were utterly spoiled by the incredible meal with the finest of everything laid out on the table. At the end of the night, the businessmen toasted all of the Massawans who had joined them for the meal, thanking us for their hospitality and announcing they would be flying back to Italy on their private plane the following day.

I breathed a sigh of relief. And no, I didn't keep in touch with Alberto or even give him my home address. I knew my dream man was yet to arrive in my life and when he did, I knew it right away.

The Deputy Commander and the Emperor

There was One Month in the Year in which Massawa would be completely transformed and the lives of its inhabitants would be turned upside down as the population tripled. The air was constantly filled with excitement as people from around the world to come and witness the spectacle that is Navy Day. An initiative of Emperor Haile Selassie, the military war games would see naval ships descend on Massawa from all corners of the globe. All of Massawa would get caught up in the festivities. The light poles would be dressed up for the occasion, as if it were Christmas, and bold flags would wave proudly in the breeze.

One by one, warships would start arriving, clamouring for a position near the naval base in a channel that was still operating commercially. Those who were not quick enough would have to set their anchors down in the open sea near the lighthouse.

Although the horrors of war were not foreign to those who live in Massawa, the presence of so much military firepower only served to boost the celebrations because all of these ships and their sailors were there in peace, as a mark of friendship. Sailors from many nations would come to Massawa to mingle and we all anticipated the official Navy Day and the Emperor's annual parade.

Between the ages of four and six, I lived a stone's throw from the Coptic Orthodox Church, where Emperor Haile Selassie went to worship. The itinerary for Navy Day was always the same. The Emperor would be driven in a majestic convoy down the main streets with thousands of people waving flags and cheering.

Police would be placed at regular intervals to control the flow of traffic as well as maintain order and the rumble of dozens of motorbike engines signalled the parade convoy was approaching. Whenever I felt the ground begin to vibrate, I would make the most of my small stature and squeeze through to the front of crowd so I could see everything.

The Emperor would make his way to his church for a ritual prayer with the priest. People would gather at the square, around the church and on the avenue that led directly to the palace all dressed in their finest national dress. Even the priest would wear his most elaborate multi-coloured robe. Everyone was beyond excited to see the Emperor, even if it was only for a fleeting moment. In fact the name Haile Selassie, which Ras Tafari Makonnen took upon becoming the Emperor, translates to *Might of the Trinity*.

The Emperor remains etched into my mind with a permanently furrowed brow and a look of intensity on his face. It was all I could see of him through the car window on his way to the palace. Like people of the Commonwealth would bow to Queen Elizabeth II, we afforded the same prestige to our Emperor. Living behind the towering walls of his white palace, he was an all-powerful figure in my mind. Someone to be both feared and revered in equal measure. As the Emperor's great-nephew Asfa-Wossen Asserate wrote in a biography released in 2015, Haile was– *unapproachable; he was the King of Kings, Abbaba Janhoy, the Great Father of the Nation, and everyone around him would bow and prostrate themselves as a sign of their great reverence for him.*

As a child, I would imagine what it would be like to live as an Emperor behind those majestic walls. So many questions swirled through my mind as I would see the palace in the distance from the veranda of my home. I was so curious how he spent his days.

Many years later, in 1969, the Bazaar closing time was approaching. There weren't many people around at 8pm, with most residents already home for the evening as was the usual state of affairs. My assistant, Abdalla Ezi had started to close and we were going through the usual routine of this time of night when two cars pulled up directly in front of the shop.

With two big doors looking out onto the street, the shiny black cars filled up the whole frame. I could see Abdalla stiffen slightly as he looked nervously at what was happening outside. I was too young and naïve to think that we could be on the cusp of being robbed. I guess I was still very innocent back then and had felt nothing but safe and secure in Massawa, so my mind would never have thought such things.

"Eufrasia, come close to me," Abdalla said, with his eyes still fixed at the windows.

"What's up?" I asked with my usual bubbliness.

"I'm not really sure... just stay close," he replied, almost in a whisper.

I took a few steps to stand next to him and we watched as the front passenger door opened and a formally-dressed man with purpose in his stride made his way to the shop door and opened it up. His face was stern and when he spoke, his voice rang out with a powerful tone that addressed me as if I was a cadet in military school.

"Signorina, his Highness Deputy Commander Iskinder Desta is outside, he needs something from this shop. Please close the doors so he can have privacy."

Abdalla and I looked at each other in awe. We had seen many wealthy and famous people in the Bazaar before, but never royalty! He was the son of Princess Tenagnework, Haile Selassie's daughter, and was born in Addis Ababa, Ethiopia, in 1934. He was forced into exile, along with the entire imperial family, when he was just a year old. Iskinder grew up in Bath, Somerset and was educated in the United Kingdom and went on to represent the Emperor, his grandfather, at many royal events such as the 500 year anniversary of the death of Prince Harry the Navigator in Spain and the wedding of King Baudouin and Queen Fabiola in Belgium. He had a reputation of being a progressive person and was a widely recognised Imperial Ethiopian Navy officer.

Abdalla and I leapt into action as the messenger returned to the second car and opened the passenger door. Because I had only ever seen the Emperor and his military personnel in their uniforms, I pictured the grandson of the Emperor to be someone who was always dressed in his finest attire – something befitting of royalty. But Iskinder was dressed casually.

I lowered my eyes as he entered the store and said, "Your Highness, welcome to the Bazaar. How can I be of service to help you with what you need?"

He looked at me and smiled, "For you, I am only Commander, no Highness needed." This took so much pressure off my shoulders and I realised I could be myself around him and didn't have to roll out the red carpet and provide silver service.

He told me he was looking for a gift for a party he would be attending the following day, so I showed him around and offered suggestions on things that might fit his purpose. One of the options was a stunning Murano glass vase. Crafted using specific ancient techniques passed down by generations of master craftspeople on Murano Island in Venice, Murano glass creations are world-famous. Unsurprisingly, this vase was one of the most expensive items in the shop. Our conversation went to Italy and I was relieved we were so at ease with one another. The prince knew that every creation of Murano was unique, and he wouldn't find a better gift in Massawa. He was escorted back to the car as one of his staff paid for the vase and the convoy left abruptly.

Abdalla and I were left awestruck by what had just happened.

Now that we had met in person, I noticed the Deputy Commander the next time I went to the Yacht Club. He was tucked away in one of the secluded corners of the venue and I waved to him. A smile of recognition spread across his face and I took it as an invitation to say hello. Although he was based in Addis Ababa, I would see him when he was in Massawa. The familiarity became such that I would simply walk up to his table with a casual, "Hi Commander, it's nice to see you." The relaxed environment at the Yacht Club meant we were both relaxed and could enjoy conversations that weren't heavy, sometimes with a dozen of Hashabella's oysters thrown in as well.

He was married to Princess Sofia Amanuel with a daughter,

Princess Naomi, so our connection was definitely not a romantic liaison. I would always make a point to ask after his wife and daughter. On one occasion, he told me that if he brought his family to town, he would like me to meet them. I came to realise he was a very misunderstood person and was very different in countless ways to his grandfather. Perhaps our conversations were a welcome escape for him and a break away from the stress of his position.

I came to value the times we shared together and one day when John was with me at the Yacht Club, I had the chance to introduce him to the Deputy Commander. Shortly after, I was invited to attend the official Navy Day Gala Dinner as one of Iskinder's guests. It was such an honour.

The Gala Dinner was held at inside Naval Base and marked the final day of the month-long event. The morning after the dinner, the military ships would take off once again and Massawa would be back to its calm, relaxed and enjoyable life for another year. This invitation would allow me to be a part of this prestigious event for the first time. I had heard so much about the event from the ladies that were all frenetic about what to wear in previous years as they spoke to me in the Bazaar. They would dress up in Chanel, Dior and creations from all of the major designers in order to put their best foot forward and make an impact. They would carry on for weeks afterwards, discussing who was wearing what label and whether they were able to pull it off. I decided to wear something classic and chose a cocktail dress in brocade green embroidered with gold roses. I completed the look with a black Paco Rabanne bolero to shelter me from the breeze and the cold of the evening and the open-air event.

I felt like a princess when I arrived at the base, even though I was late. Everybody had already taken their allocated seats and the program was underway, with someone presenting a speech from a small stage. I was captivated by the view out to sea. Lights twinkled everywhere from the naval ships of all of the visiting countries, which were in formation near the base. The stars in the clear sky were like chandeliers over what would ordinarily be a bland naval base square. Looking at the women in beautiful gowns and the men dressed in their ceremonial military suits, I had to pinch myself to make sure I was really there.

The wild dreamer still laying within me couldn't believe I wasn't there because I was famous, I was there as a guest of the Emperor's grandson! Not wanting to disturb the proceedings by trying to find my allocated seat, I ended up sitting down with a table with another young woman, who was engaged to one of the Ethiopian officers. There were also a couple of Italian officers and once the speeches concluded, we all had a great time joking and laughing.

A tap on my shoulder came out of nowhere and I spun around to see a man I hadn't met before.

"Excuse me Signorina, I am the Deputy Commander's secretary. If you follow me, I will show you to your allocated seat in the VIP area."

I looked at my watch and saw the evening would be coming to an end soon and realised people were already leaving their tables to say their goodbyes.

"Thank you for the thought," I said politely, "But I will be leaving soon, so I will stay here."

The man nodded, although looking a bit confused at me turning him down and left quietly.

The Navy Day Ball is an event I will never forget, and it was with great sadness that the last time I saw the Deputy Commander, it was with my new husband by my side in 1970 and I was announcing that we were leaving Massawa the following year. There was sadness in his eyes as I told him we were moving.

"I understand, but you are young...." he replied. There was a lot of meaning in that for me. "You will eventually come back. When you are ready, just let me know," he added.

I never did see Commander Iskinder again. He was executed by the Derg (officially the Provisional Military Government of Ethiopia) in 1974 after they overthrew the Ethiopian Empire.

Rest in Peace Commander Iskinder.

The One

I was Seven Years Old When I First Laid eyes on Gianni *John* Gagliardo. Far from the romantic comedy movies where you see someone, and your heart is all aflutter and it is love at first sight – I couldn't stand him. Given what you have read so far, you will know there is much more to John than my first impression of him!

I was playing at a friend's house while visiting Asmara when I first met John. He was thirteen years old and my overt joy and desire for adventure seemed to rub him the wrong way as he was more of an introvert, very softly spoken and openly annoyed by my loudness. As young children tend to exaggerate, I had decided that I *hated his guts* and would avoid being around him.

We crossed paths many more times over the years and

as our rotations around the sun grew in number, – that childish disdain began to fall away and we became fond of each other. John would visit Massawa regularly for holidays and special events with his family. Ever the gentleman, he would often escort his sister Francesca to the Yacht Club and whenever I was there, he would ask me for a dance.

When I became the manager of the Bazaar, I was required to visit Asmara to order and collect supplies for the shop and John became the manager of one of our suppliers. We would engage in small talk and begin to learn more about each other. Still, there was no changing the fact we were very different people with polar opposite personalities. I loved being around people and would talk to anyone, while John remained very quiet and reserved. I believed he was born in the wrong era and would have been much more at home in the 18th Century!

John's family used to go camping at Ghergsum Beach, an idyllic location north-east of Massawa. The golden sand beach seemed to extend forever out to the horizon and the waters that lapped the shore were as clear as a glass vase. Without any residents, you could enjoy long solitary long walks. John was even more intrigued by Ghergsum because there were a number of large coral dunes that jutted out of the sand and the ancient formations, which were once submerged many centuries ago, were ripe grounds for excavating fossils.

John made many interesting discoveries during low tides and whenever he got tired, he would lie down and sunbake. When the stomach began to grumble, there was an abundance of pipis he could take back to the campsite for his parents to prepare *spaghetti alle vongole*.

As the sun was setting, sometimes on the horizon, the silhouettes of Rashaida on their camels would appear. The Rashaida are the smallest ethnic group in Eritrea and are descendants a tribe of ethnic Bedouin Arabs. They live a nomadic lifestyle and historically herd camels and goats, however the Eritrean Rashaida also made a living as black market merchants.

At night-time, with nobody around to disturb you, John's family would either venture out on the water on the lampara or simply stay at the campsite and tell stories around the bonfire, which would only ever be interrupted by a curious gazelle or two.

During one of my visits to Asmara, John and I caught up for our usual *frappe* at *Latteria Asmara*, where he told me that he was leaving his position as the assistant manager of The Arabian Trading Co. and was moving to Massawa.

John decided that he would concentrate on running his own shipping forwarding agency in Massawa as he was getting tired of travelling back and forwards between our two cities. He asked me if I had any plans for the rest of the weekend, and asked me out on a date to the movies!

I even surprised myself as I immediately agreed to go with him to Cinema Corso open air movies. As the days passed in the lead up to our date at Massawa's open-air cinema, I began to get excited. Something seemed to fall into place as we sat side-by-side that night and we felt a connection that hadn't been there before.

We began talking regularly and getting to know each other better and found we shared several things, including a love of the sea. John had a large two-berth boat and we would set off with the assistance of a few sailors to Dissei Island, which is on the outskirts of the Dahlak archipelago and was two hours on the water from Massawa. Because Dissei was uninhabited, it was a wide open paradise just ripe for exploration. John loved it because he would spend the day diving and spear fishing, while I preferred to stay on board and relax on the boat and watch the sea life from above the water. The hours in this blissful location would pass by in a flash and on our way back to Massawa, we would be greeted by a glorious sunset.

We decided to get engaged rather quickly and when John asked for my father's permission, his only condition was that we had to be engaged for one year. John had begun a university degree in accounting and had let his study take a back seat as he focused on his job. He only had a couple of exams left to go before he would be qualified and I knew his professor, who had urged me to convince John to finish his study.

So I approached John with a proposition of my own.

"While I'm preparing everything for our wedding, I would like you to give me a special gift...."

"What is it?" he asked.

"Go back to study and I would like my wedding gift to be your framed university degree that we can hang on the wall in our home."

He smiled and obliged, giving me the very wedding gift I had asked for. I was so pleased that he was able to complete his degree and not have it become a *what if* in his life.

During our 365-day engagement, I discovered how much of a traditional romantic my fiancé was as he sent me a bunch of twenty-two red roses every single week and I never grew tired of receiving the bouquets.

We were married at Saint Francis Church in Gherar on November 8, 1970 in front of 100 guests, which included many of the people mentioned in this book. I had initially planned to have the wedding in St Mary's the church my father helped to build, but it was undergoing renovations at the time. A hairdresser and makeup artists had travelled in from Asmara to prepare me for the big occasion and John's best man, Filippo Cicoria, was tasked with ensuring he didn't run away before we could say *I do*.

Camillo, my best man, dressed up for the occasion in a white Panama suit with a hat, of course, to cover his baldness. There was a last-minute rush when our priest fell ill, and we had to find a replacement. Our priest was a skilled musician and was going to play the organ for us, but our replacement did not have the same talent. This meant we also had to find an organ player at the eleventh hour. This is when the karma of my hospital visits to

Signor Bonifacio came back to repay me. His son was able to come and play *Ave Maria* at our wedding, completing the ceremony we had dreamed of.

Our reception was held at the Red Sea Hotel, which was on the site of the former C.I.A.O.O.. The hotel I had daydreamed about had been demolished by that time, but its replacement was elegant and equally as popular. It was such a beautiful day and I was exhausted by the time we cut our five-tier cake.

As our married life began, it became even more clear to John that while he was very by-the-book, I would sometimes push the boundaries. One example is how I managed to drive around Massawa without ever getting a driver's licence! I had my bike and never had the desire to buy a car. There were buses we could use, but if I had to travel long distances, I would borrow John's car instead. It was one of the hottest cars around – a Chevrolet super sport red convertible with a black top. John had bought it from an American and upgraded the stereo system, which was avant-garde for those times. When I was behind the wheel, I felt like a Hollywood star. I would have the music blaring loudly and heads would turn as I drove along with my hair flowing in the breeze. While I loved how people would part like the Red Sea whenever I drove to church, unfortunately, this also drew the attention of the police. They were less than impressed by my noise pollution. I came across an officer directing traffic one sunny afternoon with the top down and the latest Italian pop song blasting from the speakers. He recognised me because the Bazaar was opposite the police station. He pointed at me and shook his head and I imagined him saying I will catch you one day!

Doing something like that would never cross John's mind and I often marvel at the things I have done in my life before strict rules began to become the way of society.

Our friends, on the other hand, had secret bets going on how long our marriage would last. They simply couldn't see how two completely different personality types could co-exist for a lifetime without getting sick and tired of each other or constantly fighting because of different points of view. But here we are, fifty-one years later still happily married and with a beautiful family that fills us both with so much joy.

For one of our milestone anniversaries, John presented me with a beautiful ring that was set with a white pearl and a black pearl on the opposite side, very similar to a Yin and Yang design.

"The white is for the happiness you have given me so far and the black is for the not-so-happy times," he said.

Not everything has been perfect and beautiful, but we have found a balance with each other and with our life together.

The Leprosy Crusaders

*A man with leprosy came to him and begged him on his
knees, "If you are willing, you can make me clean."
Jesus was indignant. He reached out his hand and touched
the man. "I am willing," he said. "Be clean!" Immediately the
leprosy left him and he was cleansed.*
Mark 1: 40-43

From the Dawn of Time, the Fear of the leprosy in humans has been palpable. The World Health Organisation says leprosy once affected every continent on earth and it has left a legacy of fear due to the history of leprosy sufferers being subject to physical mutilation from the bacteria and the consequent rejection and exclusion from society as a result.

Even though the bacteria that causes leprosy, *M. leprae,* was discovered in 1873, the first treatments only appeared in the late 1940s. This meant there was a population of people suffering from leprosy on Massawa that continued to live in a state of exile and poverty as I was growing up.

Whenever someone was suspected or diagnosed as having leprosy, they were no longer able to live in the city. Whether they left of their own accord as they understood that's what society expected them to do, or if they were cast out, I do not know.

What I do know is that they were essentially left to live in the wilderness and left on their own to survive. They either lived out in the open or were fortunate enough to find small huts to live in, although they had no electricity or access to running water outside of townships. Occasionally, I would see people with leprosy venture into the streets dressed in torn and dirty clothing with red spots visible on their skin. They would sit along the side of the streets begging for money. Without the ability to work, it was the only way they could survive.

I noticed the lepers would often be the ones avoiding eye contact and even crossing the street, so they were not in close proximity to the rest of the residents in town. They avoided people at all costs and only came into town to beg and to bathe in the sea when the streets cleared out and everyone was in their homes.

The families of some of the outcasts would do their best to care for their loved ones from a distance. They would put together packages of food and clothing and place it somewhere they knew it would be found by the intended recipient. They were too afraid to deliver it in person. Although these lepers would have felt cared for, they were still socially isolated from their family and friends, forced into a life of solitude. There is no doubt they would have suffered emotionally as well as physically from this disease. It was distressing for the families too. The only way they knew their loved one was still alive was if their care packages were collected and no longer there the following day.

The saviour of lepers in Massawa arrived when Italian doctor Carlo and his beautiful wife Sylvia were accepted by the government of Massawa to set up a missionary clinic to support and treat those suffering from the disease.

Dr Carlo was not large in stature, but he had a stocky build that gave him a strong look. You would often see him wearing khaki shorts and a white colonial-style shirt. His wife was the same height, but much slimmer and as the nurse of the clinic, she was often wearing a white smock with her long brunette hair tied up in a ponytail. When she wasn't wearing her uniform, she would wear simple skirts and tops and was elegant in her fashion simplicity. Just like Suor Pia, they had an aura around them and you got the feeling that God was with them all the time. Whenever they were near, you felt a sense of peace and happiness, which was helped along by the fact they were always smiling.

There was collective joy among the people of Massawa, particularly the families who put out the weekly care packages for their loved ones, that finally there would be somewhere lepers could be supported and cared for. It was a huge step towards removing the stigma and primal fear that was felt towards these people.

The couple were given a plot of land many kilometres from

the city, where they could utilise an abandoned concrete building that had fencing all around its perimeter. They wasted no time in transforming the site, diving the complex into one-bedroom units that had plumbing and running water – a far cry from the conditions many of the exiled had been forced to live in.

Residents in the complex also had access to a laundry to wash their clothes, a medical clinic headed up by Dr Carlo and gardens they could tend to in order to pass the time or simply rest in and enjoy the surroundings.

Dr Carlo and Sylvia would come to the town to buy supplies for their patients and with the chemist only a few doors away from the Bazaar, it wasn't long before I was able to meet these incredible human beings. They would drop by to collect stationary and other supplies for their clinic and we quickly became friendly acquaintances.

We spoke at length about the work they were doing and I felt compelled to do more to help. Now, this was in the 1960s, many years before the late Princess Diana changed the way the world viewed HIV AIDS patients in 1987 by visiting London's Middlesex Hospital. By shaking hands with AIDS patients, she forever altered people's perceptions and started to combat the rife misinformation surrounding the disease. But I had a similar idea. I wanted to visit the clinic and tell people about the experience so they could begin to have a greater understanding of what leprosy is and to create the start of a ripple effect to strip away the fear and misunderstanding.

My husband John would do anything for me, he has always been dedicated and supportive of me and my ventures. So when I came home with the idea that I wanted to visit the clinic to help Dr Carlo and his wife with their work, he agreed without hesitation to come along with me. I might add that at the time of writing this book, we have been married for more than fifty years. There have been some occasions where John will tell me I am *crazy and out of my mind* whenever I tell him of my ideas to act in service for others, but he always ends up jumping into the proverbial fire right along with me.

Just as I had visited Signor Bonifacio in the Asmara hospital as a young girl, I became a regular visitor of the clinic. At first, I would spend time with patients as they had no visitors other than the doctor, his wife or the nurse they were able to add to their team. They could have interactions with someone else from the outside world and forget their troubles for just a moment.

Dr Carlo requested that I rally the town for surplus supplies and things that people no longer needed. It could be something like a perfume that has sat unused on someone's bathroom shelf for months, or an extra bag of lollies someone is able to buy during their usual grocery shop. Being able to gift these things to the patients would give them some worldly possessions to enjoy after being forced to leave everything they had behind.

"We want to help them to feel human again. To give them back their dignity," Dr Carlo said to me and he sounded just like Suor Pia, which tugged on my heartstrings and compelled me to act.

As I knew so many people around Massawa, it was easy to get the word out that these donations were needed and it wasn't long before a steady stream of supplies, gifts and second-hand items were being given freely to the clinic and its patients.

I felt so much peace in my heart that John and I had made a difference. As the years passed, other ladies rose to the fore as the primary connections for the donations to make their way to the facility.

Dr Carlo and Sylvia raised their baby boy in their facility, further showing their commitment to breaking down the stereotype of what it meant to live alongside leper. When we left in 1971, Massawa was a community where lepers were considered human beings who deserved respect and support.

Conclusion

THE JOURNEY CONTINUES

Lord, our Lord. How majestic is your name in all earth.
Psalm 8:1

THE YEARS I SPENT IN MASSAWA WERE ONLY THE beginning of what would go on to become a rich and fulfilling life. John and I left Eritrea in 1971 with our first baby, Luigi, in our arms and our second child, Mariangela, already in my womb.

While there was a village on Taulud to help my parents to raise me, I went on to raise three children without the village. Moving to another continent as a young bride with a small child was a daunting experience. However, I had faith in our path and went on to travel the world with John and the children as my husband spread his entrepreneurial wings.

The beginning of our life adventure saw us land in Australia for a brief time in 1972 where we welcomed Mariangela into the world. In 1975, we moved to Nigeria where John became the administrator for a large Italian consulting company before launching his own company as well. John-Paul was born a few years later, when visiting Australia again on an extended holiday in 1979, completing our family. As the kids grew older, I re-entered the workforce as a teacher for grades one through to eight.

From Nigeria, we relocated to Italy, where John worked with multinational companies in Italy and saw him travelling throughout Europe, the Middle East and Mediterranean countries. It was this role that sparked a passion for working with these beautiful raw materials that come straight out of the earth. So when we moved to Australia in 1986, he had all of the skills to establish the family business that continues to thrive today.

We founded *Mar Gra* in 1986. An abbreviation of marble and granite, our business directly imports natural stones like marble, granite, travertine and onyx which is sourced from around the world and manufactured to fit customer's requirements at our base in Caloundra on the Sunshine Coast in Queensland.

Over the years, our family has been fortunate enough to have enjoyed many holidays to locations around the world. Every new location provides a source of wonder and gratitude for me and these are two qualities I have instilled in the growing generations of my family.

Until the Covid-19 pandemic, John and I had been splitting our year between our idyllic home in Umbria,

Italy and the beachside town of Caloundra, where our three children now live. The dual lifestyles filled my soul and I look forward to the time when we can go back to that once more. In the meantime, I adore being a dedicated Nonna to my four grandchildren.

When I am not helping to run the business and caring for my family, my hobbies include reading, writing, growing orchids and horse riding. Although I no longer swim or dive, I continue to gain great pleasure from being near the sea.

Writing has been a passion of mine since I was a young girl and I still have many tales to share about the extraordinary life I have lived. This book is just the beginning....

Acknowledgements

My life would not have been what it was if not for the upbringing my parents gave me. Thank you Mum and Dad, who watch over me from heaven, for all of the memories we made and all of the lessons you taught me. It has all combined to make me the person I am today.

Thank you to Suor Anna Clara and Suor Anna Carolina, my boarding school teachers and substitute parents while I was being educated in Asmara. Your kindness and wisdom have remained with me always.

To Signora Teresa and Suor Pia, you showed me how to be a strong, independent woman. Your modelling of how to give without expectation and to find ways to help others in any capacity, no matter how small, has allowed me to enjoy true connection in all of the communities I have lived in.

Thank you Roxanne McCarty-O'Kane for guiding me through the book journey and helping me to put this

Acknowledgements

together. Thank you to Aishah Macgill, my publisher, who created this book that I love.

Thanks to Raffaella Galli and Piero Traversi for helping me with the photos.

Luigi, Mariangela and John Paul, your love, support and advice is a pillar of strength for me. I am blessed that God chose me as your mother.

Lots of love to my beautiful grandchildren Gianni, Carla, Giorgia and Aurora, every day I am grateful to be your Nonna.

To my husband Gianni, your love has completed my life and you have given me so many more adventures than I ever could have imagined. Thank you for being my partner and best friend in life.

References

Massawa City. Wondermondo: The Wonders of the World. Retrieved on April 5, 2021 https://www.wondermondo.com/massawa-old-city/

Addison E Southard. Eritrea: A Red Sea Italian Colony of increasing interest to American commerce. Special Consular Reports No 82, Washington Government Printing Office, 1920.

Discover the Asmara-Massawa Road: Eritrea. Easy Voyage. Retrieved on April 6, 2021 https://www.easyvoyage.co.uk/eritrea/the-asmara-massawa-road-963

Isais Tesfazghi, Underwater Cultural Heritage in Eritrea. TesfaNews, June 15, 2019. Retrieved on April 6, 2021, https://tesfanews.net/eritrea-underwater-cultural-heritage/

Kurt Lubinski, Massawa, Eritrea: two Somali women eating outside; one covers her face to ward off the 'evil eye'. Date 1940-1960. Welcome Collection. Retrieved on

March 6, 2021 https://wellcomecollection.org/works/cfm7czct/items?langCode=eng&canvas=1

John Darnton, Eritrean Rebel Army Set for Decisive Test. New York Times, July 11, 1977 p1. Retrieved on April 6, 2021 https://www.nytimes.com/1977/07/11/archives/eritrean-rebel-army-set-for-decisive-test-eritrean-rebel-army-is.html

Valentina Donato and Sharon Braithwaite, Italian ambassador died in gun battle in DRC, not execution, prosecutor says. CNN, February 25, 2021. Retrieved on March 17, 2021 https://edition.cnn.com/2021/02/25/africa/italian-ambassador-death-gun-battle-intl/index.html

Michael Johnson, Trisha Johnson, Eritrea: The National Question and the Logic of Protracted Struggle. African Affairs, April 1981: 80 (318).

Benjamin Valentino, Final Solutions: Mass Killing and Genocide in the Twentieth Century. Ithaca: Cornell University Press, 2004.

Woman of the Red Sea (1953) IMDB Database. Retrieved on March 18, 2021 https://www.imdb.com/title/tt0045480/.

Farewell to Lino Pellegrini, correspondent and photojournalist. Oggi Trevisio, September 25, 2013. Retrieved on March 24, 2021, https://7fpqrd5yurromupn7eux7oroim-jj2cvlaia66be-www-oggitreviso-it.translate.goog/addio-lino-pellegrini-inviato-fotoreporter-70875

Arthur L McMahon Holy Sepulchre. In Herbermann, Charles (ed.) Catholic Encyclopedia. Robert Appleton Company, 1913.

Addison E Southard. Eritrea: A Red Sea Italian Colony of increasing interest to American commerce. Special Consular Reports No 82, Washington Government Printing Office, 1920.

Hemingway in Africa. Zurukenya, June 5, 2015. Retrieved on March 24, 2021 https://zurukenya.com/2015/06/05/hemingway-in-africa-2/

Rachel Nott, The history of antique mother of pearl and how to start your collection: The lustrous lining in seashells became so highly prized it was harvested throughout the world for centuries. Homes & Antiques, February 19, 2020. Retrieved March 24, 2021 https://www.homesandantiques.com/antiques/the-history-of-antique-mother-of-pearl-and-how-to-start-your-collection/

Sos Nazaryan, What is Mother of Pearl? Everything you need to know. Laguna Pearl, February 13, 2019. Retrieved on March 23, 2021 https://www.lagunapearl.com/blog/2019/02/13/what-is-mother-of-pearl/

Definition of Tornio in the Italian-English dictionary. Cambridge Dictionary retrieved on March 24, 2021 https://dictionary.cambridge.org/dictionary/italian-english/tornio

Britannica, The Editors of Encyclopaedia. Victor Emmanuel II. Encyclopedia Britannica, updated March

10, 2021. Retrieved March 23, 2021. https://www.britannica.com/biography/Victor-Emmanuel-II.

FAO Fishery Country Profile – Eritrea. FID/CP/ERI Rev 1, June 2002. Retrieved on April 6, 20201 http://www.fao.org/fi/oldsite/FCP/en/ERI/profile.htm

Marisa Crous, Eritrea's Dahlak Archipelago Islands are so remote, there's no tourism. Traveller24, June 2, 2019. Retrieved March 22, 2021 https://www.news24.com/news24/travel/eritreas-dahlak-archipelago-islands-are-so-remote-theres-almost-no-tourism-20190602.

Efraim Karsh, Neutrality and Small States. Routledge, 1988 p 112.

Britannica, The Editors of Encyclopaedia. Haile Selassie I. Encyclopedia Britannica, retrieved on March 26, 2021 https://www.britannica.com/biography/Haile-Selassie-I.

Asfa-Wossen Asserate, King of Kings: The Triumph and Tragedy of Haile Selassie I of Ethiopia. Haus Publishing, 2015.

David H Shinn, Thomas P Ofcansky, Iskander Desta (1934-1974). Historical Dictionary of Ethiopia. Scarecrow Press, 2004.

Harold G. Marcus and Donald Edward Crummey, Socialist Ethiopia. Encyclopedia Britannica, retrieved on March 26, 2021 https://www.britannica.com/place/Ethiopia/Socialist-Ethiopia-1974-91

Kjetil Tronvoll, Mai Weini, a highland village in Eritrea:

a study of the people, their livelihood and land tensure during times of turbulence. Thomas Leiper Kane Collection (Library of Congress. Hebraic Section). Red Sea Press, 1998.

Leprosy: the disease. World Health Organization. Retrieved March 17, 2021. https://www.who.int/lep/leprosy/en/

How Princess Diana changed attitudes to AIDS. BBC NEWs, April 5, 2017. Retrieved on April 6, 2021 https://www.bbc.com/news/av/magazine-39490507.

www.ingramcontent.com/pod-product-compliance
Lightning Source LLC
Chambersburg PA
CBHW021145080526
44588CB00008B/229